Ski Tips

Ski Tips

The Skier's Guide To The Perfect
International Holiday

ANDY STEGGALL

TVS

Boxtree

To Caroline

First published 1990 by Boxtree Limited

Text © Andy Steggall 1990

Illustrations © Boxtree Limited 1990

Cover Design by Dave Goodman/Millions Design
Design by Julia Lilauwala
Illustrations by ML Design
Typesetting and origination by Bookworm Typesetting, Manchester
Printed in Great Britain by The St Ives Group Plc
for
Boxtree Limited
36 Tavistock Street
London WC2E 7PB

British Library Cataloguing in Publication Data
Steggall, Andy
  Ski tips.
  1. Skiing
  I. Title
  769.93

ISBN 1-85283-282-7

Contents

Picture credits

The publishers and author would like to thank the following
sources for use of photographs on the pages listed:

cover picture Nevica, page 2 TVS, page 3 Premier Neige, pages 4, 6, 7, 8, 9,
10 Kandahar Ski Club courtesy of the Ski Club of Great Britain, page 13
Dynastar Look Nordica, page 17 Snow & Rock Sports, page 19 Dynastar
Look Nordica, page 21 Dynastar Look Nordica, page 22 Snow & Rock
Sports, page 24 Intasun (left), page 24 Snow & Rock Sports, page 25
Intasun, page 28 Top Deck, page 30 Intasun, page 33 Horizon, page 40
Horizon, page 42 Intasun, page 44 Intasun, page 48 Horizon, page 51
Intasun, page 52 Intasun, page 54 Intasun, page 55 Nevis Range
Development Co plc, page 57 Intasun, page 59 Intasun, page 63 Intasun,
page 65 Intasun, page 67 Intasun, page 72 Intasun, page 75 Intasun, page 78
Rossignol, page 80 Nevica, page 80 Dan Delacroix, page 83 Snow & Rock
Sports, page 85 Dendix Gem, page 86 Intasun, page 88 Intasun, page 94
Horizon, page 96 Top Deck, page 99 Horizon, page 101 Horizon, page 103
Intasun, page 107 Horizon

Acknowledgements

My thanks to: Phil Smith, Managing Director of The Ski Company, BASI trainer and the best ski instructor in the world; an Amstrad PC which remembered everything; David Goldsmith, Ski Survey's equipment expert, and the Ski Club of Great Britain, whose advice has been immeasurable; Gary Wardrope and Neilson Holidays for resort information; and Stuart Nimmo and the Ski Tips team who have made the last few winters such an education.

Introduction

Those who have not tried skiing will not be persuaded by flowery prose, those that have been skiing know exactly what it is like, and those who have been and dismissed it are beyond salvation anyway.

Although I am a self-confessed sports addict, it was not until about six years ago that I decided to have a go at skiing. For a long time my inertia was based on pure scepticism about a highly dubious and unnatural activity. How could anyone persuade me that it was pleasurable to strap two planks to my feet, probably with an arctic blizzard raging, and hurl myself down a mountain, no doubt breaking something in the process?

The experience was a revelation, however, and I will probably always count the first holiday as the best. I still do not know if my ribs hurt because of the odd tumble or, more probably, from laughing too much. Though the first faltering steps felt absurd, nevertheless the sense of achievement was immense. For your average athletically incompetent beginner, there is a beguiling fact which comes to light: that even over a week there is a fair chance of considerable progress, from being inept to a reasonable degree of efficient control. Enough certainly to get round the resort, away from the nursery slopes, onto the gentle runs up in the mountains – where once seen the views are never forgotten.

Many quite rightly view their skiing much as a rambler does a good walk – with refreshment stops a crucial concern! For others it is about feeling anxiety and beating it, about sensing elation and loving it. For there is always that sense of physical achievement in conquering another degree of difficulty, be it a new ski turn or a steeper slope.

At all times, though, it is important to ski safely, to take notice of the highway code of signs and instructions which the ski patrols provide for our benefit in all resorts. Going in ignorance of the dangers of the mountains can be, and has been, fatal. It is of course an extreme environment, even if, treated with respect, it is also a paradise. During the filming of the TVS programme "Ski Tips" the ski patrol at Les Crosets in Switzerland was persuaded to detonate an avalanche for our cameras (with us at a safe distance of course). In fact *pisteurs* set off mini-avalanches regularly; it is a precautionary measure to clear them away in a controlled manner, before an overload of snow becomes too dangerous to lives and property in its path. On this occasion the sight was truly awesome: full-grown conifers were plucked out of the ground and flung down the mountain as if they were matchsticks. I am glad I have seen an avalanche in safety. As a mere visitor to the mountains, it was a thundering reminder of what the mountains can do.

The "Ski Tips" presenters, me and Liz Wickham, just before our balloon ride over the Rockies.

Interview at 10,000 feet! The "Ski Tips" crew filming on the slopes. The camera crew members are all able skiers which certainly comes in useful on the piste.

You can never learn enough about the mountains, but then you can never have enough of the fun they offer either! Indeed making the "Ski Tips" programme has been a highly fulfilling arrangement, allowing me to indulge some of those boyhood ambitions which were otherwise likely to remain only dreams – from the shuddering exhilaration of a 70 mph "plummet" with the British bobsleigh team down the Olympic run at Innsbruck, to the pure romance of a balloon ride over the Rockies. On top of this, there has been the thrill of working with a dedicated film team who regularly defied the intimidating logistics of shooting in extreme conditions of snowstorm and cold. And then there have been all the people we have met on our adventures: the cowboys who ski in Colorado; the British woman doctor who learnt to ski as an old-age pensioner (and now attends race camps at the age of 67); the flamboyance of the snowboarders and freestylers; the matter-of-fact skill of all the ski instructors we have met in every country; the bonhomie of stylish French restaurateurs and Austrian mountain bar owners.

Stunning scenery, plenty of thrills and great conversation add up to an irresistible combination. So coming up in the next few chapters – some distilled thoughts on how to get the most out of a wonderful obsession!

Snow, sun and an exhilarating sense of freedom as you fly down the slopes.

CHAPTER ONE

History

Most of us are relative newcomers to skiing – swept along in the recent wave of enthusiasm for the sport. But there is no doubt that skiing possesses a long and fascinating history; and it is one in which the British have played an interesting part, even if we have produced little in the way of record-breaking successes in recent years.

Of course, the beginning of man's achievements on snow go back to prehistory. An archaeological find is in fact the first evidence we have: the Hoting ski, dug out of a Swedish bog, and now housed in one of Stockholm's museums. Just one metre long and 20 cm wide, this piece of prehistoric carpentry dates back to approximately 4,500 BC. Two further skis and a ski pole, dating from 500 years later, were found in Sweden at Kalvträsk in 1924.

These early skiers, found carved in rock in north-west Russia, are thought to date from approximately 1,000 BC.

Also from Scandinavia comes a third find, probably dating from 4,500 BC as well: two rock carvings of men on skis, discovered in Norway on Rödöy Island. As for manuscripts, Chinese texts from AD 626 mention skiing, while from 1205 there are documents telling of the rescue, by a band of skiers, of the future King Håkon of Norway. But if the odd artefact and a few ancient manuscripts do not immediately fill you with the urge to grab your skis and head for the slopes, then some of the characters from more recent times may help bring the pastime to life.

In the 1830s the Norwegian General Bierch became a driving force, and inspired the first open cross-country, or *langlauf* race. It was guaranteed to have good snow conditions because the event was staged near the town of Tromsö – more than four hundred miles inside the Arctic Circle! Indeed Norway and her emigrés were to be fundamental to the world-wide spread of the sport. They even travelled as far afield as Australia, forming what is believed to be the world's first ski club at Kiandra in the Australian Alps. Meanwhile on another continent "Snowshoe" Thompson was striding across the Sierra Nevada in California, regularly using skis to deliver the mail. The Norwegians were in America following the Gold Rush, and dispensing their knowledge as they went; and it was via America that they gave the initial impetus to Swiss skiing. For in 1868 Giacondo Dotta returned to Switzerland from a gold digging expedition, and took with him the first pair of skis ever to be seen in Switzerland.

There, we know, the new pastime was soon taken up by the travelling British: for while thwarting Victorian villainy in the pages of his Sherlock Holmes stories, the author Sir Arthur Conan Doyle also had time to take up skiing at Davos in 1889. But in the meantime the different topography experienced in central mountainous Europe was also bringing changes in ski technique. Cross-country skiing was ideally suited to the rolling terrain of Norway; but on the steep slopes of the Alps different technical elements were required. In 1896 a mini ski revolution began with the publication of *Lilienfeld Skiing Technique* by the Austrian Mathias Zdarsky. Not only did he modify the existing equipment (making the skis shorter, adapting the bindings and using only one pole), but he also established the very first "ski-school". Through his theories, an early version of "snow ploughing" replaced the accepted telemark turn.

Now enter the holiday business in the unlikely shape of a party of British Methodist Ministers, who were taken to a conference in Grindelwald by Henry Lunn. This first "package holiday" dates back to 1898. Just five years later, on 6 May 1903, the Ski Club of Great Britain was born, or rather toasted into being over dinner at the Café Royal. In true sporting tradition, it was not long before the British organized the first international downhill race: run at Montana in Switzerland on 7 January 1911, and set up, again, by Henry Lunn. Twenty-four competitors started out in a *kerschmossel* start (all together) from above the Plaine Morte glacier – much to the incredulity of their Swiss hosts. The race became known as the "Roberts of Kandahar", after an army general, famous for his feats of bravery in Afghanistan, who had given his name to the cup for the winner. There was no prescribed course, the aim was simply to get from top to bottom of the mountain as quickly as possible. Ingenuity of navigation, and an eye for a short cut, were all part of the test. If British expertise has waned, relatively, in recent decades, the name of this first race still lives on. The World Cup race at the Austrian resort of St Anton is recognized as one of the blue-riband events of the winter season. With a good snow record it is usually held before Christmas and is still called the Kandahar.

An early Roberts of Kandahar race in 1927. Skiers Ford, Joannides, Mackintosh and Riddell hurtle down the slopes.

Back in the early 1900s Kandahar racing was taken to a number of mountain villages in Switzerland and Austria. Soon other races followed, like the "Inferno" at Mürren, still the longest downhill race in the world. Here one of the winners, in the course of an illustrious ski career, was James Riddell, past President of the Ski Club of Great Britain and vice-Captain of the British Olympic team in 1936. But he admits his elation at winning was tempered by the absence of the judges at the finish line. James, with skis still on his feet, entered the nearest hostelry to find the committee quaffing ale. If they were startled at being found out, it was nothing to their astonishment at Mr Riddell's winning time which was some three-quarters of an hour quicker than the previous year. How racing has changed what with the difference between success and failure measured these days in hundredths of a second.

Transport to the start line has changed too. Nowadays there is every modern mechanical convenience to whisk the courageous to the top of the hill. Then, however, the only way to the top was to climb. Competitors would set out at dawn, rucksacks filled with sustenance for the coming exertions, and it would then take most of the day to reach the starting line. Of course if the weather was inclement or the effort of the climb weighed too heavily, Mr Riddell and his fellow racers had to seek alternative means of competition. Fortunately one understanding hotelier allowed time trial attempts down his spiral staircase. But their host did take exception when the racers opened out the feather contents of a duvet on the stairs, to add extra realism to the scene.

The Lunn family continued to have a major influence on ski competition. In 1913 it was Henry's son, Arnold Lunn, who suggested the first rules for downhill skiing, in a publication called *Skiing*; while in 1922 he was responsible for shaping the rules for slalom racing, when the British organized the Alpine Ski Cup and the first slalom race at Mürren. Meanwhile women were establishing themselves in the new sport. British women formed the Ladies Ski Club in 1923, followed by the Swiss shortly after.

An early ladies' ski team in the 1930s – note the rudimentary bindings.

However, the dress etiquette of the day made few concessions to their pursuit of the outdoor life. Bulky crinolines and flowing skirts were still deemed appropriate. At the same time equipment generally was still very basic. The crude wooden skis were considerably longer than today's designs, while cable bindings were, in many skiers' view, more of an injury threat than a protection. Nevertheless important developments were being made by the 1920s in ski technique. With Hannes Schneider's establishment of the "Arlberg" school at St Anton, there had evolved what has been seen as the first modern ski school for holiday-makers with graded classes.

By 1930 the tourist business had taken hold and the idea of the winter holiday was catching on. So much so that Sestrieres in Italy became the first purpose-built resort. But skiing as a major competitive sport had also arrived. In 1931 the first world championships were held at Mürren in Switzerland. (The women's title was won by Esmé Makinnon of Britain, so among the ladies, at least, British skiers were still at the top.) A year later skiing finally achieved Olympic recognition, when at Lake Placid in 1932 the Nordic disciplines of ski jumping and cross-country were given full status. Four years later Alpine skiing received similar acceptance, in the 1936 Winter Olympics at Garmisch-Partenkirchen, with downhill and slalom events for the first time. In the following years it was skiers from the highland countries of

Timekeepers at Innsbruck in 1933

Scandinavia and Central Europe who continued to take the lead in competition and in innovation of ski technique. None more so than the Austrian Anton Seelos, who was not only an incomparable world champion, but is also credited with developing the parallel turn.

By the 1930s there were also major improvements in ski-slope transport. In 1934 the first T-bar drag lift was opened in the Swiss resort of Davos, while in Wengen the skiers persuaded locals to extend the railway up to the hamlet of Kleine Scheidegg. The "Downhill Only Club" had really come of age, as skiers revelled in the opportunity of taking a train to the top! Two years later, on another continent, the first chair lift was opened at Sun Valley, Idaho, in the USA. These new lift systems not only improved the lot of the skier; they were also the catalyst for a new generation of ski resorts. Up to this time ski resorts had always grown around some existing facility: health spas, or popular summer resorts or villages and towns renowned for mountaineering. Fundamentally what all the original ski resorts shared was direct accessibility by rail. Now, just as the pressure of numbers was increasing on the pioneer resorts, these new devices appeared to speed skiers up the mountains. This meant that villages in much less obvious locations were opened up to an income through ski tourism – especially since designs like the T-bar required relatively little investment.

Joannides (centre) racing at Mürren.

After the Second World War, the development of skiing quickly resumed, both in tourism and technical innovation. In Austria an impetus to tourism came from an unusual quarter. In 1946, at the instigation of America, the Marshall Plan was mounted, to revitalize countries ravaged by the war. The Austrians decided to use the aid to develop tourism, and embarked on an ambitious programme of building ski lifts and hotels. Meanwhile, in technical terms, 1948 was a double landmark for British inventiveness – as always spurred on, perhaps, by our own lack of top-grade skiing. The expertise of a furniture manufacturer, Donald Gomme, of G-Plan fame, resulted in the construction of the first wood-laminate metal-edged ski; while another famous High Street name, Lillywhites, opened in London the world's first dry ski-school.

The carved sculpture on the table shows the cumbersome dress women skiers used to wear. This was presumably a fancy dress race, judging by the false beards the timekeepers are sporting.

But it was to be another fifteen years before the first artificial ski slope was built by Dendix. Its lattice pattern of plastic bristles has become perhaps the epitome of British ingenuity in skiing without snow. Also still to come were the third generation of European resorts: the purpose-built centres which have become famous in France, and infamous among architectural traditionalists. In earlier years the French Alps had been better known among exponents of climbing. But these new creations, of the

1950s and 60s, changed all that. Untroubled by existing settlements or lines of communication, their designers started from scratch – literally scraped and moulded their creations with explosives and bulldozers. President de Gaulle became a figure-head to the cause, while the likes of La Plagne, Les Deux Alpes, Les Trois Vallées, Les Arcs and L'Alpe d'Huez became reality. These are skiers' resorts, with lifts and ski runs to your front door; and if they do not have the atmosphere of their more traditional counterparts, it still means nevertheless that there is all the more choice for us the skiers.

So we come to the 1990s – and what comes next? There is much soul-searching among the skiing community, as more becomes known about damage to the environment: acid rain, pollution from exhaust fumes, the simple denuding of slopes through an excess of people in the mountains. Already, it has been estimated, the Swiss Alps have lost 30 per cent of their foliage, from one human cause or another. Perhaps we will find that this is the decade of the "green skier".

CHAPTER TWO

Equipment

Boots

Ski boots are your single most important item of equipment. On them can depend the success of your entire holiday – and, at the beginner stage, whether skiing becomes a passion for life or an uncomfortable experience and an equally painful memory. A recent survey of first-time skiing holidays which were felt to have failed suggested that in 30 per cent of cases it was put down to ill-fitting boots. But with proper guidance, and with the recent huge technical advances in the design of ski boots, there is really no need for any aches and pains. Whether you buy or hire, the range of types can be bewildering. But the vast majority of beginners start with a rear-entry boot; and since, if you are buying, you should probably think of spending £130 or more, you want to make sure they fit.

HOW THEY WORK
It would in fact seem a fairly impossible task, for the human foot with its infinite peculiarities to survive within a massive plastic shell; especially when it may be locked away for a day at a time. But the purpose of the boot is serious enough: to provide the essential link between you and the skis. So a boot's design will aim to give the lower leg a "forward lean", to stabilize the ankle for protection, and it will try to help your control over the skis by limiting any sideways flex of the ankle. (Note though that a boot should never be so tight that it impairs the ankle's ability to flex forward and straighten through 30°–45°.)

There are two main varieties of boot: rear-entry and front-entry. Front-entry are still the preference among many advanced downhill skiers and even some intermediates, but for most people rear-entry boots have become by far the most popular choice in recent years.

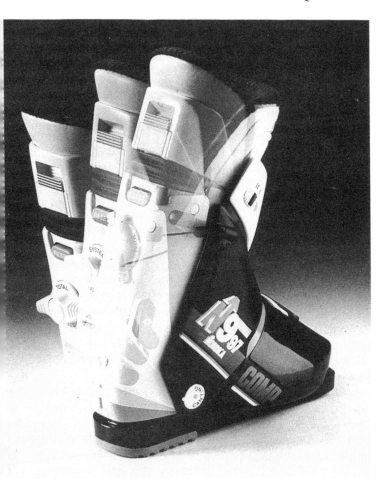

The rear section of the boot opens backwards for comfort and ease of fitting. The boot is then adjusted using a system of cables.

Rear-entry Boots

Rear-entry boots have virtually taken over in the 1980s, and that is due quite simply to comfort and ease of fitting. On these boots the rear section opens backwards. Depending on the manufacturer there may be a variety of ways to adjust the fittings, and these also allow the boot to be "half opened" for an extra stretch when resting, or to make walking easier.

The boot has several components which give the closeness of fit. In the rear-entry boot a cable running inside the shell and across the instep (the highest part of the foot) is the major element holding the foot and heel down. When the boot closes it is important that it fits closely round the cuff. There are generally other controls and elements aiding the closeness of fit, and the more you pay the greater the range of levers; but however many there are make sure you never tighten them too much, especially at the start of the day. The foot should always be given time to settle into a boot.

Front-entry Boots

Also known as "clip boots", these are the traditional design. A shell covers the top of the foot and is secured by a series of clips, so holding the foot firm. Clip boots are still the equipment for Alpine racers, and many other skiers beyond beginner level also prefer them for the control they give.

Buying Boots

If you decide after the first one or two holidays that skiing could become a winter fixation, then the first piece of specialist equipment to buy is definitely boots. However, the quality of ski slopes and their ability to fit boots can vary drastically; so it is most important to be satisfied with the shop assistants who are giving advice. Equipment manufacturers are just as concerned that good advice is given, and many have provided courses to instruct counter staff in how to help you.

First and foremost – it takes time. Realistically you cannot make a decision in minutes about footwear which will be in constant use for many hours. Good shops will expect you to take it slowly; I have known friends take a book to read while their feet are getting accustomed to their owner's choice. One or two shops have even offered a cup of coffee to pass the time! Some shops will allow you to take a pair of boots away to try on a dry ski slope. If your skiing is outpacing the quality of your ski boot then there are shops which will offer a reasonable trade-in on your last pair.

Here are a few points to note when buying boots.

1 Be prepared with a proper set of socks of the type you would wear while skiing. Make sure they are long enough to come above the height of the boot cuff.

2 Your normal shoe size is only an indication. Many boots are graded on volume. The fitter should also be looking at the height of the instep and width of the foot.

3 Your toes should touch the front of the boot when standing straight, but as you adopt the skiing stance with your legs flexed there should be more space.

4 Be a little cautious of boots with lots of foam padding and extra attachments. While this may be the perfect solution for some

people, it is just as well to try another manufacturer whose range may give a slimmer fit.

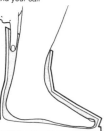

Checking for fit before fastening the boot, press your ankle foward; there should be room to insert a finger between the back of the boot and your calf

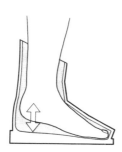

A fastened boot should allow no upward movement at the heel

...nor if you stand on tip-toe should your toes press hard against the end of the boot

Customizing Boots

However many knobs some people have to twiddle they are never satisfied, and there are various ways to customize a standard boot for a perfect fit. First there is the foamed inner boot: foam generated from a chemical reaction between two fluids is forced through tubes beneath the boot shell and into a bladder in the inner boot. Orthotic inner soles are another device. These are heated and then the feet are placed on them; once they have moulded to the feet they are left to cool and harden into shape. Finally there are inner linings which can be cut and shaped to comfort with an electric grinder.

> Dominate your equipment. Your skis and boots will do as little as possible if you let them. Learn to master your equipment and be athletic.

SKI TIPS

Skis

know from experience that when I was a beginner my skis felt more like a hindrance than a help! It wasn't too bad heading in a straight line, but any thought of turning was quite out of the question. Skis, however, have been designed to turn, to bend and twist, and given just a little bit of help they really can take a lot of effort out of the headlong rush down the mountain.

DESIGN

A few technical advances in ski design are made each year but most changes are simply cosmetic variations on the basic structure. The tip and the tail are curved, and both narrow in to the middle section of the ski, called the waist. In profile the ski has a camber, with the highest and thickest point again in the middle. Down the underside is a central running groove. A cross-section through the interior of a modern Alpine ski would reveal a fine collection of mostly high-tech materials. The majority have a foam plastic and/or laminated wood core, and there will also be layers of glass and carbon fibre (and perhaps even metal fibre) in various forms and combinations, to create strength and dampen the effect of vibration on the ski. Reaching the outsides again, the top and sides will be hard plastic, the base (underside) polyethylene and the base edges hardened steel.

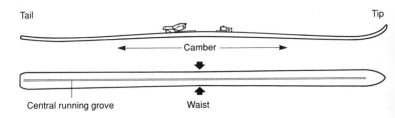

Tail   Tip

Camber

Central running grove   Waist

What is important to you though is the outcome of all this expertise: what the ski does when you put your foot on it and how the design enables you to control the movement. Two features in particular make wearing a ski different from strapping a length of floorboard to your foot. These are the camber and the waist, both at the mid section. Without them, ski techniques would be very different. In fact, anything other than an uncontrolled slide in a straight line would be almost impossible. It is the raised camber which makes a ski dynamic rather than dead, flattening to touch the snow as your weight is applied, flexing away again as your weight passes to the other ski. So the ski feels alive and responsive to your movements.

Just as important is the side cut, which is the name for the narrowing towards the ski's waist. As the ski's camber flattens, edging your ski to one side impresses the curved side cut into the snow, so your ski turns. I have heard it likened to a train on a curved railway track.

Buying Skis

The quality of most skis from most manufacturers is very high, so perhaps it's just as sensible to pick the ones which go best with the new ski suit. In any ski shop there is always an earnest customer flexing skis. I know, I have done it. But the experts will tell you that there is so little difference between quality general-purpose skis that it is a waste of time, even though it may look professional. Admittedly, Austrian skis tend to be a little bit stiffer than French ones, and there are powder skis which are much softer than those meant for icy conditions and pisted skiing. But by the time you come to buy skis, rather than hire them, you'll know if you mostly ski piste or powder. And beyond that it's really just a matter of taste.

Consider carefully whether you should hire or buy skis; as a beginner or intermediate skier your rate of progress will be rapid and you may soon require a different length of ski.

If it's going to be the first pair you've bought, get a budget package which will also include the bindings. But make sure the bindings are of relatively superior quality to the skis, because the skis may not last very long (either through wear and tear or

because your ability will outstrip their usefulness) but the bindings will. Ascertain the right length of ski for your standard. It is not worth buying skis when you are a real beginner because your progress will be so rapid, necessitating longer skis. When you start out a rule of thumb is to have skis which come up to head height or a little shorter (about nose height if you are beginning on dry slopes). Thereafter, as you progress, you go up in increments of 5 cm. As a comfortable length, somewhere over 10 cm above head height is where most recreational skiers end up, with 20 cm above the limit for the expert holiday skier. But if you are overweight for your height, then you need skis a bit stiffer than others of your ability; and if you turn out to be a real boy (or girl) racer, or the next world speed record holder, then there are skis which are 2.4 m (8 ft) long.

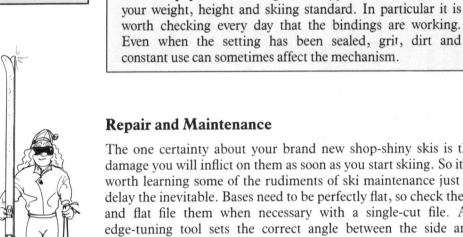

SKI TIPS

Whether skis and boots are your own or hired, make sure that all equipment is the right size, type and adjustment for your weight, height and skiing standard. In particular it is worth checking every day that the bindings are working. Even when the setting has been sealed, grit, dirt and constant use can sometimes affect the mechanism.

Repair and Maintenance

The one certainty about your brand new shop-shiny skis is the damage you will inflict on them as soon as you start skiing. So it is worth learning some of the rudiments of ski maintenance just to delay the inevitable. Bases need to be perfectly flat, so check them and flat file them when necessary with a single-cut file. An edge-tuning tool sets the correct angle between the side and bottom of the edge. When conditions are icy, sharp edges make a lot of difference. Inevitable gouges and holes will appear in the base, and these can be "P-Texed" – i.e. the damage can be masked by dripping molten P-Tex (heated by a burning candle) into the scratches. Once it has set you scrape the base smooth. To wax skis, smooth molten wax over the base with an iron and scrape down to a smooth finish.

Rather like taking the car in for a service, the life of a ski can also be prolonged with a trip to a good ski shop, where many of the above procedures can be carried out more expensively but possibly more expertly, using machinery designed especially for the job.

Bindings

Just sometimes there are days on the slopes when the slightest miscalculation will see you and your skis taking separate scenic routes down the mountain. This is where bindings come into their own.

One of the most important developments in recent years has been the progress in the design of bindings. Once they were little more than cable contraptions which literally bound the legs to the skis, quite often with unfortunate consequences for the skier. Today however the release binding is a simple and effective piece of engineering, which nevertheless manages to fulfil a number of tasks. It handles wear and tear, icing and impact, yet is still capable of releasing the boot when it "senses" undue pressure through the leg. The boot is bound to the ski by two units, at the toe and the heel, with the boot locking between them. The binding will release in the event of excess pressure being exerted on the mechanism, e.g. during a fall. But it also has the job of absorbing the shocks encountered during a controlled run, over perhaps rutted and icy terrain, without causing release.

Improvements in binding design have increased the safety of skiing immensely. Most bindings work as two units at the heel and the toe.

To achieve this, the DIN setting (devised by the German standards organization) is crucial. This is a numerical setting somewhere between 1 and perhaps 15. Manufacturers have charts to determine a person's DIN setting based on his height, weight and skiing ability. It's worth buying a good quality binding so that as you progress you are not forced to buy new bindings as well as new skis. On the other hand, buying the very top of the binding range is not necessarily a good idea, because essentially you are paying for a stronger spring which gives a higher level of performance but no greater level of protection. In consequence, the numerical scale on such a binding could begin on a number above that which is sensible for your level of skiing near the middle to top of the range shown on the binding. Downhill racers ski on something above DIN 15, and the speed skiers on the Flying Kilometre would usually have bindings set at around 25.

Bindings range in price between £50 and £130, and all those sold in Britain will have passed independent standards, so there are no major differences in safety between them. The differences occur in the directions in which the boot will release. Some toe bindings will release upwards as well as sideways, in the event of a twisting fall. Also, while all heel bindings will release the boot upwards in the event of a forward pitch, only a few will release in the event of a fall straight backwards. One other important part of the construction is an automatic device, the ski brake, which releases two prongs into the snow to slow down the speed of a runaway ski. Make sure these are working properly when you take to the slopes. After a fall, a ski travelling some distance down the slope isn't just inconvenient, it could also cause serious injury if it were to collide with skiers below.

Ski Poles

Relative to other items of equipment, choosing the right ski poles is a simple business. There are just three criteria: the right length of pole, the type of hand grip and the weight.

The basic guideline for length is simple. Hold a pole with upper arm dropped towards the waist and forearm held out horizontally. The distance to the floor is then about right. Remember though, that if you cannot carry out this experiment in the snow you must make allowance for the extra couple of inches below the basket (a plastic disc to stop the pole being pushed too far into the snow). This tip is of course supposed to grip into the snow, so to compensate in a ski shop you hold the pole upside down and work out the comfortable working height by gripping the pole just below the basket.

There are two basic grips. One has a strap, with or without a moulded grip to give a snug fit for the fingers. Make sure there is a safety provision so that, in the case of a very hard fall, the strap will detach itself from the pole. If it remained fixed there could be painful repercussions for the fingers. The other style of grip is the sword grip, with a plastic shield round the back of the hand. These are perhaps less fiddly yet the strap grips far outsell them.

The most common type of hand grip is a strap; when choosing poles make sure the strap has a release mechanism in case of a very hard fall.

If you are skiing on a dry slope, do not use the straps.

Poles should possess some resilience and strength, but they do not want to be too heavy; no one wants to go weight lifting while they are skiing. Light poles are better than heavy ones and aid posture and stick action.

Clothes and Accessories

The next best thing to choosing a ski holiday is choosing the ski wear to go with it, and it is a big operation when you consider that you need everything from underwear to sunglasses. It could also be expensive if you need to kit out the whole family, and in some cases it is a shock to find that the prices are as dazzling as the designs. Like all things, however, you get what you pay for, and this is where high street fashion and high technology meet head on. The manufacturers will tell you that ski clothes are the most complicated forms of garment you can buy. A lot of development time goes into new designs, not only at the fabric stage but also at the manufacturing stage. It is more like engineering than "haute couture", as the garment makers strive to find the most satisfactory process which works – part of the reason why some clothes cost so much.

Skiing buzz words can be pretty startling and a rummage through the shop hangers will find you grappling with high-tech jargon to match the high-tech materials. Don't be surprised to come across names like Gore-Tex, Tactel, Entrant, Super Exeltec, Cyclone, Super Microft. As with other outdoor activities, skiing has seen a Holy-Grail-like pursuit for an ultimate fabric which will be both waterproof and sufficiently breathable to allow perspiration to escape; plus, if possible, both hard wearing and inexpensive. The original ideas were based on microscopic holes but now it is all changing. This year there are fabrics on the market which work by chemical reaction, the fabric being coated with an amino-acid polymer to react with the perspiration.

This ski suit has a high collar and is roomy enough to allow ease of movement. A hat that covers the ears and good gloves or mittens complete the outfit – and you are ready for the slopes.

At this end of the market one outfit will cost well in excess of £500, and you are already heading down the slippery slope to a huge credit-card bill. For the individual or the family, there are other ways of going about keeping warm, looking good and still having the price of a hot chocolate and rum after the last ski run of the day. Many budget-conscious shops are competing in the market, catering for everyone from toddlers to grandparents. So for the price-conscious, here is a guide to the essential ski wear ingredients.

SKI TIPS	Ski length. As a rule of thumb, skis should reach head height for beginners, or nose height if you are starting on dry slopes. As your standard improves, ski length can increase in increments of 5 to 10 cm. If you want to be a speed skier get the tape measure out – 8 ft is a decent length!

The head loses more heat than any other part of the body (about 25 per cent of total heat loss). So buy a close-knitted ski hat: preferably wool, though acrylic is perfectly adequate, but it must come down to cover the ears. For the body and neck a standard piece of ski wear is the cotton roll-neck shirt. Build layers up, and the warmer you will be. One or perhaps two T-shirts under the roll neck are a good idea, as well as jumpers (preferably light with a high wool content). If you can ski with a small rucksack over your shoulders, then you also have a means of reducing any of those layers if you are getting hotter or the temperature changes. Remember the weather conditions can change dramatically in the mountains and it is better to be prepared for the worst, however sunny it may seem from the hotel window in the valley floor first thing in the morning.

Non-ribbed socks are important, with reasonable wool content, and long enough to come above the ski-boot shell. Trousers come as padded dungarees (or salopettes), racing pants or ski jeans. Salopettes have the advantage of full protection round the waist; but whichever you chose, make sure the legs fit over the ski boots to stop determined snow flakes getting in, and that there is room to do the splits (it can happen).

When buying skis for the first time, ensure the bindings are of a quality which will allow you to re-fit them to your next pair of skis. As you progress, your standard will outgrow ski length long before the bindings are worn out.	SKI TIPS

The major investment will be a ski suit, or a jacket to go with ski pants or salopettes, and here you must come to some compromise perhaps between high-fashion looks and function. Check to find out the strength of the fabric and the quality of the stitching on the seams. Look for double stitching around the most vulnerable parts of the garment where most pressure is exerted, e.g. across the shoulders and under the crotch. Look for plenty of pockets in the right places so it's easy to get to sunglasses, piste maps, suntan cream, lift passes and the rest of the paraphernalia you'll probably be taking. Are the zips easy to use with ski gloves on and are they an anti-freeze design? Many jackets have hoods attached; they are not essential, but if you want one as an option check it can be tied efficiently and encloses all of the head. Make sure the garments are roomy to allow plenty of clothes underneath, and give you plenty of scope to bend and stretch. There is always a debate between the advantages of an all-in-one ski suit and the two-piece trousers and jacket. If you spend most of your time in the "deep and steep", a ski suit does stop most errant snow flakes finding their way into some of the more uncomfortable parts. On the other hand if the sun shines you can gently boil in an all-in-one; and when it comes to a well-earned rest at a mountain watering hole there are a few more tribulations as you try to divest yourself of a few layers or try to seek relief!

There is nothing worse than cold fingers. While you are skiing you probably won't notice until you come to the long chair lift ride back up to the top! Experts will tell you it's not worth skimping when it comes to buying gloves. A jacket does not have to be the most expensive because you can make up the deficiencies with extra layers, but with gloves it isn't possible to take the same line. Leather gloves are the strongest, or there are some composite materials combining water-resistant fabrics. If you opt for the latter make sure there are leather reinforcements around the thumb, forefinger and palm at the very least. If the edges to your skis are sharp anything less than leather will be ripped to shreads. For those who really get bitten by the cold it is worth considering mittens, and there are also inner gloves (using aluminium or silk).

(left) Children can have fun whatever their age, but make sure they are wrapped up well against the cold. This toddler's clothing is multi-layered and a warm rug offers further protection from the low temperatures.

(right) Cool sunglasses for bright light. Protect yourself from the glare of the slopes by investing in good quality sunglasses. Remember to attach them securely, with either a strap around the neck or with clips around the ears.

Sunglasses or goggles are essential, to protect eyes from the intense ultra-violet light in the mountains. Goggles are best for fog and flat light, and for skiing in powder, or while it's snowing, because they can enhance the definition of the terrain. Make sure they are double lensed. Though all goggles are prone to misting up, double-lens glasses are far less afflicted by this tiresome occurrence than the single-lens variety. You can get yellow goggle lenses for mist, brown for sunshine. But when the sun starts shining, most people will be wearing sunglasses, and a high-factor sun cream: it is very easy to burn.

CHAPTER THREE

Resorts

A button lift ride to the top of the world. Skiers reach the summit of the run by being pulled up on seats which are suspended from a cable on long metal rods.

There have never been so many ski holiday options as now, and somewhere among all the glossy brochures is the right one for you. But how do you set about picking a holiday – what should you look for?

Most British skiers tend to go to either Austria or France, but with over four hundred resorts in Europe alone the scope can be bewildering. You may well go on recommendation. But whether you are holidaying alone, in a group or with a young and demanding family, the right choice will be fairly crucial. For most of us the excitement of a winter holiday begins with an armful of the new season's glossy brochures. Flicking through these pages is an art in itself. The temptation is to pick a resort by price alone. But while it is pointless picking a holiday that is too expensive, it is also frustrating to arrive at a resort only to find it has the wrong grades of slope. Study the brochure maps carefully, and borrow the piste maps if you can for the area you are likely to choose. Green and blue runs are for beginners, reds are for intermediate and experienced skiers, black runs are for experts. This is a vital clue to the suitability of a resort.

Detailed maps may help pinpoint your accommodation, and it is worth checking that, after the last run down, you are not still faced with a marine-like "yomp" to the luxury of a hot bath. Much information can also be gleaned from the better travel agents. Ask to speak to the skiers on their staff. Some companies, like Neilson, run ski-training courses for their agents, and a badge of competence or some similar qualification will be displayed in the shop.

For a beginner the best choice is usually a fun-loving, friendly resort with lots of après-ski. The Austrian resorts are particularly noted for this. If you are flying, try to find a resort with a short transfer time from airport to destination – two hours is a reasonable average. Italian resorts do not have the luxury of a Geneva or Munich airport relatively close, and transfer times can clock up to well over four hours.

Find nice gentle slopes to begin with. Your first holiday is not about beating every Franz Klammer down the mountain. In fact it is an idea to give the big resorts with miles of piste a miss for the first holiday at least. Usually the lift passes (and ski hire) are more expensive, yet you will not be experienced enough to take advantage of what they offer. Find a resort where the nursery slopes have been allocated plenty of space; somewhere where they are close to the village, and do not double up as a major thoroughfare for other skiers coming down the mountain. The purpose-built resorts usually have the edge in this department, since they are also located high enough up to be sure of reasonable snow. Alpe d'Huez in particular comes highly recommended.

It's always worth going with a group of friends if you can, but if that's not possible there are plenty of other ways of being gregarious. Some travel agencies organize skiing groups, while tour operators are often able to offer a single person a place in shared accommodation, whether apartment or chalet. Anyway, ski resorts are sociable places, and you should have no trouble making acquaintances at your own level of skill.

Chalet Holidays

The first thing to remember about the chalet holiday is to come out to the resort with a present for the chalet girls – especially pots of Marmite and peanut butter spread. When I canvassed the opinions of some chalet girls about the treats they were missing from Britain those two came top of the list. I am sure a bottle of wine would do just as well!

If you have gone with a group of friends then the chalet, something which is perhaps unique to the ski holiday, can be a real pleasure. There is none of the formality of a hotel yet there is still the chance to be pampered and cosseted a little. The chalet girls will cook every evening (they will leave you to your own devices for one night on their day off), keep the place clean (though they are not there to wait on you hand and foot) and may also bake a cake and ply you with piping hot tea when you have just come off the slopes in the afternoon. Prices will not be a great deal cheaper than a hotel tariff, but with the right people it is something which captures the essence of the skiing life and it is certainly worth a try.

For the beginner, a week's ski school is money well spent. All reputable ski schools are geared up to making the most of your holiday. Even if the learning process becomes hard going it is still a great way to meet new people, and after the first faltering basics have been mastered ski instructors will be only too willing to show off the best views in the resort as well as teach (it is a holiday after all).

Ski School

For all beginners ski school is a must, not only as a way to enjoy your holiday to the utmost but also to be safe. It is quite likely that beginners will be going on their first holiday with a tour company well versed in novice predicaments i.e. the process of getting the right ski pass, hiring the correct equipment and finding the appropriate ski class.

It is still quite daunting heading for the initial lesson. On the first morning there will be lots of people and lots of organized chaos; just watch and listen and with the help of your tour rep and the English-speaking instructors it will all be sorted out surprisingly quickly. If you are a real beginner then there is no point worrying – just leave yourself in the capable hands of the instructor (well versed in the flustered misgivings of the rank beginner) who will take you through the early steps. To begin with there will be lots of uphill side-stepping followed by a smooth slide down the gentlest of gradients. There are lots of basic exercises to get you acclimatized to the strange objects on your feet and to give you some idea of the possibilities they hold. What soon becomes apparent is everyone's capacity to improve. A gentle free slide can soon have some control exerted on it. By the end of the first day, you will have grasped the rudiments of the snowplough and the basic turns.

A ski class for beginners. Ski school provides an excellent opportunity for learning to ski correctly and safely; it is also a great way for making new friends.

SKI TIPS

In order to alleviate anxiety, never ignore the most obvious solution: finding another route on which you would feel happier. Recognize your ability level. It sounds simple but often people feel goaded into following friends, and the consequences are sometimes painful. An important aspect of the victory of mind over matter is setting realistic goals based on your skiing ability at the time.

Others, who have had the forethought to go to the local dry slope for lessons or who are regular winter holiday makers, will have to go complete a ski school test. They can be pretty tense affairs on your first morning. As you set off, you suspect that every pair of Bolles and Ray Bans on the hill are focused on you. Of course the ski school does need to get some idea of standard ("intermediate" covers a whole miscellany of styles and abilities) and with a large number of people to organize it can be a bit hit or miss. It is worth helping your cause by getting a couple of runs in before the test even if it does mean an early start. If, after a couple of days, you think you are not keeping up with, or are getting ahead of, the class standard then don't be afraid to ask for a change. A class size should not exceed about ten. The other option is private lessons but they tend to cost a lot. A two hour session could cost you perhaps £50. If two or three of you get together to split the cost, then the benefits of individual attention will soon become apparent.

On rare occasions the skiing bug can just pass some people by! So think about a resort which will have enough to occupy those who ski and those who do not – as well as those who need a day's rest. You should try to avoid a resort without adequate lift capacity, especially during school and local holidays. Who wants to be queueing when you have paid to ski? The simple solution is to pick a resort which is small and relatively isolated. Some of the big resorts are victims of their own success: for example, the internationally renowned Kitzbühel. Meanwhile Val d'Isère (equally well known) has fewer queues at peak times, after massive investment in its lift system, which now includes a funicular railway. High in the Tarentaise, it is also difficult to get to, so only the more committed and patient try – though major road improvements in time for the 1992 Olympics will change all this.

To improve your chances of finding good snow, especially early in the season, book a high-altitude resort. On average every 100 metres' vertical rise corresponds to a temperature decrease of one degree Celsius; and the colder it is the better the chance of snow. Certain resorts have a reputation for snow before Christmas, including Val d'Isère (famous for its downhill race, the Première Neige), Verbier, Hintertux, Selva and St Anton. Prices are "low season"; though so, realistically, should be your expectations of the skiing conditions. Certainly over Christmas and New Year the ambience and festivities are as important as the skiing, which is the reason why the British have been heading to Mürren for years.

Falling. Do not be afraid of falling. Everybody falls. When you take a tumble, try to sit back and fall to one side. Just before touching ground, straighten the legs to avoid any twists.	SKI TIPS

Through the bleak early weeks of the New Year experts say you should ski on mountains predominantly in the tree line, where visibility is better and more shelter is afforded. The weather in recent years has produced a rather barren mid-season period, with much of the best snow coming later each year. At the end of the season, from late March into April, look for resorts with plenty of north- and east-facing slopes, and consider Scotland which comes into its own at this time.

As for accommodation, there is always a balance to be struck between cost, convenience and atmosphere. Should it be traditional or purpose-built; self-catering or hotel? If you are the single-minded skiing type, or with a young family in tow, then function is the primary concern rather than original old-world charm and night-life festivities. Hence the purpose-built resorts have acquired a reputation in these fields. The action men and women have plenty of opportunity to blast their way round the ski motorways and powder fields all day and retire well satisfied at night, while the family can leave young ones in well-organized crèche and kindergarten facilities. Newly designed self-catering blocks invariably have easily accessible shops – though prices can be as steep as the mountain-top on which you are perched. One drawback is that purpose-built resorts, by their very nature, take some reaching, and with young children the transfer journey can become very arduous.

An evening of tobogganing – one of the attractions found on nearly all skiing holidays. Though beware: it is not as easy as it looks so watch out for bumps and scrapes!

In Italy and Austria the emphasis is on hotel or bed-and-breakfast facilities. Switzerland has a wide range of accommodation from basic rooms to palatial mansions. The picture postcard villages are just as much a part of skiing as the intricacies of the "stem christie" or chair lifts made for two. There are fine examples throughout the Alps from Megève, one of France's first resorts, to St Christoph in Austria and Morgins in Switzerland. But old values were changing by the 1960s, and the new mood was captured in France especially, where cuckoo clocks quickly made way for breeze blocks. The French Alps are littered with high-rise purpose-built resorts like Avoriaz. The architect here designed the buildings so that at a distance they looked like mountain and rockscape. With space at a premium they were also designed to cram as many people as possible into areas as small and tall as possible. You would be forgiven for thinking a multi-storey carpark attendant built some of them.

Note the weather before each day's skiing. Take adequate clothing with you, because conditions can quickly change. If it doesn't make you feel uncomfortable, ski with a small day sack, rucksack or bum bag in order to carry an extra sweater, hat etc.	SKI TIPS

Nowadays architectural traditions are returning, as at the French resort of Val d'Isère. They've realized that people want something pretty as well as functional; hence the re-emergence of the Savoyard farm house, built in wood and stone and with steep pitched roofs. At Val d'Isère the miracles of civil engineering are, instead, the lift systems; and if you think the cost of your lift pass is about as steep as the nearest black run, then take a look around you and wonder how the resort's mechanical cobweb took shape.

The French director of the Val d'Isère lift system, Jean-Denis Lagarde, speaks for most of his counterparts when he outlines three major objectives: no lift queues; make skiers happy and give them a good welcome; and get to know the different nationalities who come to Val d'Isère. Each year resorts will be checking where bottlenecks are developing, and planning for new lifts to make the system even smoother. Meanwhile, if we find queueing frustrating, perhaps we should bear in mind that we as skiers can probably be rather off-putting en masse. So much so that at Val d'Isère M Legarde swops his control point staff every year, to give them a rest from us. Saying hello in any language isn't a hardship, and harassed lift operators may appreciate it.

Ski Resort Choices

There is such a rich and varied range of resorts to see and ski that my initial feelings about making a few suggestions were first that it was an impossible task, and second that it was an invidious one. Some of the following would certainly stand out in anyone's list of ski-resort greats. But others, inevitably, are purely personal preferences: the scenes of some of my own most enjoyable times in the mountains.

For most people a skiing holiday will be a European one, but it does not have to be that way. Increasingly countries and places, which until now may have been only names in an atlas have come alive as the ski resorts of the future. The market leaders in Europe are of course Austria, France, Switzerland and Italy, though Scotland is expanding every year, and Eastern Europe is awakening to the opportunities too, especially in Bulgaria. But then there is the rest of the world: Japan alone boasts 600 resorts; the USA becomes more alluring to the British every season; while for those who dream of skiing when their neighbours are happy sitting on a beach, there are such distant southern-hemisphere locations as Argentina, Australia and New Zealand. Just take your pick and enjoy a worldwide obsession.

Austria

For many people Austrian style is the epitome of what a ski holiday should look and feel like. There is the picturesque wood-chalet village charm, the wholesome food and wood fire smells of the mountain restaurants, the good cheer of the "umpah" bands, the tree-clad ski slopes, and of course the meticulous Austrian ski-school instruction to the sound of "Bend zee knees". For groups of mixed ability Austria probably has the edge on any other country, with its emphasis on an all-round winter holiday. Their skiing is suited to all standards and their ski schools have a very good reputation for doing it the "correct" way. In fact the current head of Interski (the world association of ski instructors) is Professor Hoppichler from the Austrian mountain village of St Christoph, part of the huge Arlberg region. When it comes to life off the ski slopes, there is the Austrian tradition of friendship and good fellowship; and they have a name for it too, *Gemütlichkeit*. There is simply so much to do in Austrian resorts; they are renowned for their skating and curling rinks, sleigh rides, and often fitness and beauty facilities, along with indoor swimming pools and saunas. You will find that bowling and tobogganing will probably be high on a tour operator's agenda, as well as copious amounts of beer and schnapps. The following are not the only choices but they represent some of the largest and most famous (all prices are approximate).

ST ANTON

St Anton has become a real mecca for skiers from throughout the world. In any bar or hostelry, on the slopes or in the town, you will hear a very fair selection of accents. But the resort is not for the faint-hearted, with some of the toughest and most exhilarating skiing in the Alps. St Anton is situated high in the Arlberg Pass. On one side of the valley are the twin areas of Valluga and Kapall, providing a massive amount of challenging skiing. On the other side a ski-bus ride of less than five minutes from town gives access to the Gampberg ski area. A lift pass includes not only St Anton but all the Arlberg ski "circus" which includes the neighbouring resorts of St Christoph, Stuben, Lech and Zurs. For a small charge buses give easy access to these interconnecting resorts, while the bus service within St Anton itself is free.

With an established record of good snow early in the season, conditions have also been enhanced with snow-making machinery, especially on the well-used lower slopes. For beginners there are several small nursery slopes at Galzig, Gampen and on the Rendl. Since some of these locations require a cable-car trip first,

The resort of Kitzbühel in Austria offers true picture postcard scenery. It is a resort with something for almost everyone, including a village which dates back to the thirteenth century.

St Anton has provided a special "beginner's" lift pass. The lack of relatively easy slopes, though, means that St Anton is not the ideal choice for first timers. For the intermediate skier, however, the number and variety of red runs is outstanding. The higher open slopes and the lower wooded pistes on the Rendl are ideal, and at Kapall and Galzig the enormous scope makes this one of the best intermediate areas for improving any form of skiing. There are plenty of mogul fields for the flexible and agile – a mogul being a bump on the slope. Of course the moguls are not only for the average, and for black-run, expert skiers there are some of the toughest runs in Europe. Steep skiing and off-piste areas abound, together with the chance to join some of the most instructive top-grade ski classes anywhere. The high mountain runs from the top of the Valluga, especially from the Mattun and the Schindlergrat, are legendary. There is also heli-skiing on offer later in the season, while despite St Anton very much being home to the downhill experts there are also 40 km of cross-country trails.

The cost of a top hotel, for a week's half board, plus flight, will be between £380 and £600 depending on season. A pension or apartment, also with flight, will cost between £250 and £300 for bed and breakfast. The price of lift passes is approximately £70 during low season and £77 in high; a passport photograph is required.

For children there is a special junior ski school provided for those between five and fourteen years of age. The total cost including lunch for six days is approximately 1,800 Austrian schillings. There is also a kindergarten for non-skiing children (an important bonus for skiing parents), which is provided for three to fourteen year olds. It operates throughout the skiing day, and provided you are staying in St Anton there is only a charge for the older kids of about 300 Austrian schillings.

SKI TIPS	At all times take note of the piste signs and carry a piste map. Often the runs will have markers to tell you which side (left or right) you are skiing. Also the marker poles sometimes have numbers which reduce in value as you get closer to the end of the run.

Off the slopes St Anton is the epitome of the Austrian approach of providing something for everyone. Here are both the traditional and the modern; of the latter none more so than the mountain bar called the K.K. or Krazy Kangaroo, which is young, antipodean, loud and very boisterous. In the main, car-free, street there is a host of restaurants, bars, clubs and shops. If, by some unbelievable chance, you have any energy left after a day on the slopes, then there are also numerous hotel swimming pools and saunas (open, at a charge, to anyone), an indoor tennis and squash centre, ice skating, curling, sleigh rides, bowling and tobogganing.

KITZBÜHEL

This resort is located at the far east of the Tyrol next to the Schwarzsee Lake. While it is one of the most chic of ski holiday destinations, the village also lives with the dominating reminder of another aspect of Kitzbühel's fame: the Hahnenkamm, the most notorious racing mountain in the world, and home to one of the great classics of Alpine competition for more than fifty years. The cable car up the Hahnenkamm reaches the heart of the resort's ski area, while another access route is via the two Streifalm chair lifts. From their summit spring many intermediate and expert off-piste runs. There are also the ski areas of Pengelstein, Jochberg, Pass Thurn and Kirchberg, all of which are covered by the Kitzbühel ski pass. The most challenging skiing in the region is beneath the Steinbergkogel chair lift, with a 500 metre descent down a steep, north-facing, deeply mogulled run. For beginners the nursery slopes are positioned at the foot of the Hahnenkamm. The ski instructors go with the mountain – they are called the Red Devils. There is also, on the other side of the village, the Kitzbühler Horn (1,200 metres high). Here the variety of intermediate blue and red runs is enormous, though many are quite short. There are kindergarten facilities which meet at the "Disneyland" slopes (showing that the traditional can also find a place for more modern creations). They cater for children aged between four and twelve.

Kitzbühel village dates back in parts to the thirteenth century, having developed into a medieval walled town, and it is now one of the most attractive examples of Tyrolean architecture. Apart from skiing there are all the usual much loved winter-resort pastimes, including a swimming pool, the Aquarena, which is covered by the ski pass. At an extra charge you can also enjoy a solarium, sauna and mud bath! Along with plenty of cafés and restaurants there is also a casino (formal dress required). At high season a quality four-star hotel will cost in the region of £460 for a week, half board, including flight. Christmas is quite a speciality in the town, and prices rise to high-season figures even though snow conditions can be very uncertain.

SÖLL

Lots of British holidaymakers know about this one, where ski schools are English speaking, and beginners and newcomers to skiing are plentiful. The resort is famous for its onion-domed church, round which the village has developed at the Foot of the Wilder Kaiser Mountains. The main ski area is ten minutes away from the village centre, connected by ski bus, and from there chair lifts connect the Hohe Salve summit. There are beginners' passes for those who do not want to venture further afield than this; but for the more proficient, however, there is a lift pass to the whole of the Grossraum. This is Austria's largest interconnected ski area, comprising more than 80 lifts and 250 km of ski runs. From the middle station on the Hohe Salve there are direct links to the ski resorts of Hopfgarten and Scheffau. There is also access to Ellmau, Going, Brixen, Itter and Westendorf.

For intermediates and beginners alike the runs on offer are excellent, though advanced skiers will not find conditions that are very taxing (the best are found in the Wilderkaiser-Brixental area). There is a ski kindergarten for children between five and twelve, costing approximately 1,000 Austrian schillings per day. Throughout the season the Söll-only lift pass costs £47 while the all-season Grossraum pass costs £57 (relatively cheap in comparison with many other resorts). With a lower station at 621 metres and a 1,827 metre top station, the area is relatively low-lying. So if there is a paucity of snow in the Alps this area can suffer, depending on the prevailing direction of the weather.

SKI TIPS	Never ski alone, and when skiing off-piste stay in groups of three as minimum. Ensure all your party are wearing avalanche rescue devices.

Söll, with 29 km of cross-country track, also runs ski-school classes in *langlauf*. The resort, however, is as much known for its après-ski, geared very much to the young and fun-loving, and is rather more competitively priced than many other Austrian resorts. There are natural ice rinks, floodlit outdoor swimming pools (heated of course), and a 5.5 km toboggan track. From Salzburg the transfer time is one hour thirty minutes. Bed and breakfast in a village home or guest house for a week with flight comes to £169 through the low season up to a high season £240, while a hotel of perfect fourteenth-century pedigree will cost just over £400 in the premium weeks at the end of February and beginning of March.

AUSTRIA

	ST ANTON	SÖLL	KITZBÜHEL	OBERGURGL	SOLDEN
Top Station	2,650m	1,827m	2,000m	3,035m	3,068m
Pisted run	200km	250km	155km	100km	160km
Longest run	8km	6km	8km	8km	8km
Nursery slopes	9	6	10	3	4
Easy runs	34	31	34	15	6
Medium runs	70	23	28	12	30
Difficult runs	30	6	10	5	5
Total No. lifts	74	87	59	23	23
Lift pass (6 days)	£67–76	£47–57	£55–70	£70–80	£70–80
Day nursery	3–14 yrs	–	2+ yrs	2+ yrs	–
Ski nursery	5–14 yrs	5–12 yrs	4–14 yrs	5+ yrs	3–8 yrs
Transfer time from Salzburg Airport	1½ hrs	1½ hrs	1½ hrs	4½ hrs	4½ hrs

Special feature: Solden has highest cable car in Austria

OBERGURGL/SOLDEN

A contrast to Söll, as far as altitude is concerned, is the resort of Obergurgl, the highest parish in Austria, at the head of the Ötztal Valley. The top station is 3,035 metres high, and the snow record is consistently good. There are two secondary settlements close to the village, Untergurgl and above it Hochgurgl. From Obergurgl there are two other main areas on predominantly north-west facing slopes: Gaisberg-Hohe Mut, connected from the middle of the village, and to the east lifts to Festkogel. Obergurgl has wide open nursery slopes beside the village, and rather in the French style there are plenty of motorway blues and reds for the intermediates. The pick of more testing routes is the Wurmkogl black run, from the highest point in the lift system, looking out over the Italian border.

There are also cross-country trails linking Obergurgl to Untergurgl in a ten-kilometre loop. Though it possesses the customary accompanying facilities (like ice rinks, swimming pools, etc.) Obergurgl is a little way down the Austrian league for other entertainments. It is very much a skier's resort, and its snow record, which is what will make or break a holiday for the committed skier, is very good. One drawback is its distance up the mountain chain, which means that the transfer time from Salzburg is long, at over four hours. From Innsbruck, however, transfers take approximately two hours. High-quality hotel accommodation costs in the £300-£400 range, depending again on the time in the season, for one week with flight, while bed-and-breakfast chalet-style holidays are approximately £100 cheaper.

An Ötztal Valley neighbour, lower down at 1,377 metres, is Sölden, and 700 metres above it is its outpost of Hochsölden. With the highest cable car in Austria, the Ötztaler Gletscherbahn, skiers can be transported to above 3,000 metres, to the Gaislachkogl summit. Access from here leads to the challenge of a number of difficult black and red runs, and to the glacier skiing which opens up towards spring.

Prices at Sölden are similar to Obergurgl.

Switzerland

This country's level of service and efficiency cannot be beaten, not only in the ski resorts themselves but on the way to them too. The train services to the mountains from the main cities, like Geneva and Zurich, are justly renowned. When you get to the resorts they are mostly traditional in style and beautifully kept, and some are famous for their lack of motor traffic. Saas Fee, Mürren, Wengen and Zermatt have all banned cars; the alternatives are battery-powered buggies and vans or their horse-drawn equivalents. Prices can come as something of a shock to the British, but that is the cost of exceptional attention to detail and reliability, especially when it comes to the lift systems. The Swiss pride themselves on the most efficient and safest uphill transport systems in Europe, including some of the most modern underground funiculars at Zermatt and Saas Fee (though as in Austria the humble T-bar is commonplace and has been known to unseat the unwary). It was calculated recently that all the country's cable ways together can move one and a half million skiers an hour – and not many people know that!

The range and variety of ski resorts in Switzerland ensures something for everyone. Among the most famous are Wengen, Davos/Klosters, St Moritz, Verbier, Zermatt and Crans Montana.

SWITZERLAND

	ZERMATT	SAAS FEE	CRANS MONTANA
Top Station	3,820m	3,500m	3,000m
Pisted run	150km	80km	160km
Longest run	14km	9.5km	3.5km
Nursery slopes	3	4	2
Easy runs	11	10	20
Medium runs	17	14	20
Difficult runs	12	9	10
Total No. lifts	36	24	40
Lift pass (6 days)	£90–150	£75–85	£35
Day nursery	1 month–8 yrs	3–6 yrs	2–8 yrs
Ski nursery	4+ yrs	–	3–6 yrs
Transfer time from Geneva Airport	4hrs	3½ hrs	2 hrs

Special feature: Saas Fee has an underground railway and especially good mogul fields; Crans Montana has free public transport with or without ski pass

ZERMATT

In any well-composed picture of Zermatt there is one highly photogenic element which is essential: the distinctive sharp outline of the Matterhorn which overshadows the town. In fact the start of the Zermatt experience begins before you reach the resort. Not only because of the towering Matterhorn, but also because the last part of your journey is completed by mountain railway, since the centre of Zermatt is traffic free. There are three main ski areas. Gornergrat/Stockhorn is a forty minute train journey away. It offers intermediate runs in the main, plus some very tough black runs from the Stockhorn. The Blauherd/Sunegga area is reached by a three minute trip on the express underground cable railway and then by cable car or gondola. This section is famous for the national downhill course. The third sector, the Klein Matterhorn/Schwarzsee, is a fifteen minute walk or a taxi ride from the centre. For the beginner Zermatt offers rather limited facilities, though the main nursery area at Sunegga is easily reached by express underground. But the 150 km of piste should be more than enough to challenge most intermediate and advanced skiers; and if not, there is always the trip over the mountains to Cervinia in Italy.

Off the slopes Zermatt is renowned for the breadth of its activities, including helicopter trips round the Matterhorn costing approximately 150 Swiss francs per person, with a minimum of four to a charter. Other attractions include an Alpine Museum, while horse riding is available in Tasch. There are also all the usual facilities like curling and ice-skating rinks, swimming pools, etc.

Zermatt is particularly good for its care of children. The Kindergarten Theresia takes children from one month to eight years old. If they are over four years old they can take advantage of skiing facilities too. The cost for six days is 214 Swiss francs without lunch. Another kindergarten, for non-skiing two to eight year olds, is located at the Hotel Mont Cervin. As for accommodation, Swiss prices are admittedly more expensive than the average, and you can only weigh this against how much you value Swiss efficiency. At high season a self-catering apartment for one week, with flight, is around £350, while a quality hotel will be over £500. The transfer time is also on the steep side – over four hours from Geneva.

All good resorts are conscientious about catering for the needs of children. After a few days on the slopes they are usually better than their adult counterparts.

SAAS FEE

With its highest station at 3,500 metres this resort has a good snow record, while the Fee glacier ensures skiing all the year round. There are four natural areas. Felskinn and Spielboden-Längfluh are both accessible from the Mittelallalin summit and are also linked by snow cat – just one more way of lightening the burden of uphill transport, along with numerous lifts and the world's highest underground railway. The two other ski areas are Plattjen and Hannig. For absolute beginners the nursery slopes are gentle and wide; some even double as tennis courts during the summer, so they can't be too daunting! But there are also some exciting red and black runs, and the fields of the Weisse Perle offer plenty of scope for experts in "mogul bashing".

A noted feature of the resort is its spectacular scenery, while in the traffic-free village there is a high quality of service. Facilities include a very well provisioned sports centre, with indoor swimming pool, tennis court, gymnasium and sauna. There is also a curling rink, and many local walking trails that give the non-skier plenty of chance to take in the winter atmosphere. Again, hotel prices will give you little change out of £450 or more at high season. The lift pass costs £75 at any time.

CRANS MONTANA

This resort found fame with the British from the outset. At the turn of the century, from some 3,000 metres up on the Plaine Morte glacier, twenty-four intrepid Brits set out on the first official international downhill race. These racing traditions were revived in 1987 when the Alpine World Championships were staged here, and the fillip which this event gave Crans Montana can be seen today in recent huge improvements to the dual town. But the distinct identity of the two villages still very much prevails. So much so that, depending on where you are staying, you may hear the resort referred to as just Crans, just Montana, or even as Montana Crans. Crans has been a mountain home for Geneva's Swiss élite for many years. It became renowned for its chic, fur-wearing, caviar-eating image, while Montana has always been a haven for the more serious skier. Still, the differences have waned somewhat in recent years, and the integration of the two centres has turned Crans Montana into Switzerland's largest resort. Today there is a general air of wealthy sophistication about the place – especially the shops! There is a fair chance that any designer label worth its name will be on prominent display in Crans Montana.

Whatever the differences, too, all visitors and villagers agree on the beauty of the spot. The site is a south-facing plateau overlooking the Rhône Valley, above the medieval city of Sierre; and further south, as a backdrop, are the peaks around the Matterhorn.

Crans Montana's 41 lifts cover a huge ski area, including the largest glacier open to skiers in Europe, La Plaine Morte. There are only a handful of downhill runs on the glacier, which is instead a particular mecca for cross-country skiers from throughout the world and throughout the twelve months of the year. It is quite an experience stepping onto the glacier in mid summer only to be "bombed" by the whole of the Japanese World Cup cross-country team on their morning exertions . . .

Crans Montana, home of the first downhill races, and one of the most popular of Swiss holiday destinations.

In fact expert downhill skiing is not plentiful at the resort, but for intermediates it is a delight, with the combined areas of not only Crans Montana but also Barzettes-Violettes and Aminona. The three areas are well linked and accessible from four base stations, with the skiing mainly between 1,500 and 2,500 metres. There is also heli-skiing which can be arranged from nearby Chermignon.

Italy

Relaxed, informal and friendly are all adjectives which come to mind about Italy – and sometimes, admittedly, less than efficient! Among the famous resorts of the western Alps are Courmayeur, tucked below Mont Blanc, just across the border from Chamonix, and Cervinia, further down the Aosta valley and just south of the Matterhorn. Unique to Italy, however, is the change in scenery when the typical Alpine landscape of the west gives way to the Dolomites of the east. Here the resorts of Selva and Cortina d'Ampezzo are home to chic and style, with looking good in the village high street just as important as getting it right on the slopes.

ITALY

	COURMAYEUR	CERVINIA	VAL GARDENA
Top Station	2,755m	3,492m	2,950m
Pisted run	100km	180km	29km
Longest run	6km	18km	9km
Nursery slopes	4	4	15
Easy runs	9	11	52
Medium runs	13	16	17
Difficult runs	1	5	3
Total No. lifts	31	36	56
Lift pass (6 days)	£0–80	£70–75	£70–85
Day nursery	–	–	2+ yrs
Ski nursery	5+ yrs	–	4–12 yrs
Transfer time from	GENEVA	GENEVA	VERONA
nearest airport	2 hrs	4½ hrs	2½ hrs

Special feature: Cervinia has especially good intermediate runs

COURMAYEUR

Come out of the exhaust fumes of the Mont Blanc tunnel and just past passport control you drop down to one of Italy's prettiest-looking resort villages, Courmayeur. Take a walk down the high street here on a Saturday afternoon, and wind, rain or shine Italian society will also be taking their fur coats for a stroll. The food to be found among the twisting cobbled streets is superb, while for skiers the resort offers 100 km of piste stretching from the 1,224 metre base up to the 2,755 metre peaks of Cresta D'Arp and Cresta Youla. These, however, are dwarfed by the most imposing feature in Europe – Mont Blanc. Altogether there are plenty of sights and sounds vying for the lucky visitor's attention.

The main ski areas are on the sweeping plateau of the Checrouit to the north-east. To get to the ski slopes you begin with a cable car ride across the river valley. As with many resorts that rely on one major line of communication, this can be rather crowded at peak times. To save effort, however, boots and skis can be locked away on the plateau overnight. There are also the wooded north-western slopes of the Val Verny, and the three-stage Mont Blanc cable car which gives access to the infamous Vallée Blanche down to Chamonix. Included in a special six-day pass is one day's access to another famous Aosta resort, Cervinia, as well as excursions just across the border to Chamonix and Mégève.

Perched at the foot of the Matterhorn, the Italian resort of Cervinia is one of the highest in Europe.

CERVINIA

This resort is one of the highest in the Alps, at 2,050 metres, and is famous both for its snow record and its scenery. Like Zermatt it is overlooked by the Matterhorn (though in Italy this is known as Il Cervinio or Mount Cervin). Cervinia's ski area is vast with five major cableways, and the resort is a paradise for intermediate skiers. Advanced skiing, though not extensive, is still demanding. To the south of the resort the Cielo Alto chair lift serves steep and unprepared runs, and in spring the off-piste runs on the Plateau Rosa are opened up, also giving access to Champoluc and Valtournenche. There is also a route over the border to the Swiss resort of Zermatt (this costs a supplement to the basic £69-a-week ski pass). Like many of the top Italian resorts, Cervinia is famous for its gourmet food. Of course alongside its restaurants the resort centre is bustling with shops, bars and cafes, and for those with surplus energy there is an ice rink, and at Cielo Alto two swimming pools.

THE DOLOMITES/SELVA

This area was first studied by a French scientist called Dolomieu, from whom it gets its name, and in anyone's language the scenery is exceptional. It is rather like the landscape from an American cowboy film transposed, with snow, to Italy (giving a new twist to spaghetti westerns, perhaps). Large flat-topped limestone massifs dominate the horizon, and at sunset the rocks' pinkish tinges are brought to life. Along with the region's geological individuality there is a political individuality to match. After the collapse of the Austro-Hungarian empire, at the end of the First World War, the South Tyrol region was ceded to Italy. But a mere change in ownership has never deterred the mountain people of the area from going about their lives in much the same old way. The main concession to niceties of government seems to have been placenames in Italian rather than German; e.g. Selva was once called Wolkenstein. In fact for real locals even the Austro-Hungarian empire was a mere newcomer, since here one of the oldest living languages in the world, called Ladin, is still healthy and widely spoken.

Selva is located in a narrow valley, along with Santa Cristina and Ortisei. They are together known as Val Gardena, the placename given to the local World Cup race. In turn this is just a small part of the Sella Ronda, which is a ski-tourist's dream, comprising kilometre upon kilometre of interconnected routes around the most dominant feature in the area, the mountain massif of Sella. There are plenty of villages to see on the way, including Campitello, Canazei and Arabba. You can attempt the full journey, which takes in excess of five hours – not allowing for rests and lift queues! Overall the circuit offers 20 km of uphill transport and 26 km of skiing through 4,000 vertical metres. Most runs are blue, the rest are red.

Around Selva there are plenty of snow-making facilities and wide-open nursery pistes for beginners. A free bus travels up and down the Val Gardena, giving access to a number of stepping-off points into the mountains. In the town itself bed-and-breakfast facilities predominate, along with chalet-type amenities. But there are top-class hotels too and plenty of après-ski, especially restaurants and discos.

France

Though there are traditional resorts in France, the country has made its name for its purpose-built door-to-door skiing facilities like Avoriaz, La Plagne, Tignes and Flaine. They can be a little soulless, but as they have been located at high altitudes they are more likely to have good snow conditions, and they are a real boon for families, with skiing for tiny tots as an integral part of the design. With the modern construction comes an emphasis on self-catering apartments, rather than hotels, another plus for the budget-conscious family. Also in such resorts the lift systems, like the rest of the facilities, are both new and logically positioned to use the mountains to their best advantage. Making the most of the modern ability to "paint" ski runs onto the side of mountains with bulldozers and dynamite, French resorts have developed the "circus" arrangement, with integral links between a number of neighbouring centres. Ski run facilities are no longer an extension of one village, they are massive areas. The following are just some of the most famous.

SKI TIPS	When skiing on busy slopes, concentrate on the spaces and not the people. Worrying about the close proximity of a skier will probably ensure you collide with someone!

VAL D'ISÈRE/TIGNES

These two ski resorts high in the Tarentaise are jointly known as L'Espace Killy, after Val d'Isère's most famous citizen, Jean-Claude Killy, the all-conquering Olympic hero of French skiing in the 1960s. Together the two resorts (which will play their part when Albertville hosts the 1992 Winter Olympics) have 300 km of pisted run with a vertical range of 1,938 metres rising to a top station of 3,488 metres. The transport facilities include one of the newest and fastest underground railways in the Alps. In four minutes it whisks skiers from Val d'Isère's "suburb" of La Daille to the heart of L'Espace Killy and the top of the World Cup downhill route. The Val d'Isère race, the Première Neige, is in fact the first in the European calendar, which is fair testament to the resort's good snow record. From Val other routes into the labyrinth of ski runs include access via Le Joseray, close to the village centre, and two cable cars to the "Tête de Solaise", while a bus connecting Le Fornet higher up the valley gives access to the Glacier de Pissaillas. Tignes too has three main sectors: Tovière, Grande Motte glacier, and Palet/Palafour/Aiguille Percée. Generally the resorts offer plenty to challenge all grades of skier.

Neither perhaps is the most obvious choice for beginners, but both do have nursery slopes and runs suitable for even the most cautious. In the case of Val in particular it is really only that the scope is so vast that it may be difficult for the beginner to get full benefit.

Though the two resorts are interconnected by ski routes, and also share a very high standard of off-piste skiing, they are in fact quite dissimilar. Val is an old, well-established village which first opened its doors to ski tourists in the 1930s. Along with a weekly market there are something like thirty bars and ten discos, including two owned by British expatriates, Dick's Tea Bar and the Playback. Indeed the British influence has been immense – many go there and some stay! Other facilities at Val include cleared walking trails, and a fitness centre with swimming pool, gym, solarium, sauna, etc. Meanwhile Tignes is a product of the "new" architecture which typified the third-generation purpose-built resorts. It is primarily a skiers' resort and can be quiet, though there are plenty of bars and discos if you look for them. Again there is a well-equipped fitness centre if you have enough strength left.

Transfer time for the two resorts is about five hours from Lyons, or two to three hours from Geneva; providing, that is, that the traffic along the Isère valley does not snarl things up. As has already been stressed, the main difference between France and other European countries is the emphasis on self-catering apartments. Though the initial outlay for flight, one week's stay and accommodation may be relatively low, remember food is extra. Superstore prices for the basics in French resorts are not cheap – though it is a chance to try the superb local products, and in France that of course includes wines, cured meats and sausages, patisseries and cheeses. Eating out will be pricey too. For the basics, therefore, expect to pay about £150 per week at low season and at high season just over the £300 mark. For apartments catering for up to 6 to 8, prices will of course be lower.

LES TROIS VALLÉES – COURCHEVEL/MERIBEL-MOTTARET/VAL THORENS

A giant among ski areas is Les Trois Vallées, with 500 km or more of pisted runs, the longest 8 km. Many an expert would argue that even in a fortnight it would be impossible to cover every metre of this skiing playground. Meribel and the hamlet above it, Mottaret, hold the central position in the three-valley chain. To one side is the Courchevel valley, and to the other lie Les Menuires and Val Thorens, which at 2,300 metres is the highest ski village in Europe. All of them are covered by the Three Valleys lift pass (£67 at low season and £77 through the high season). Again, compared with some of the Alpine countries with a longer skiing tradition, après-ski is relatively limited, but then perhaps night life is not the main reason for coming to a skiers' paradise. In Meribel-Mottaret and Val Thorens the accent is definitely on self-catering. Apartments range between about £130 and £260 depending on the time in the season. Courchevel is split into a number of separate villages, above Saint-Bon Courchevel, differentiated by their altitudes: 1,300, 1,550, 1,650 and 1,850m.

LES ARCS

This resort is another which has been subdivided by settlement into a series of altitude elevations, Les Arcs 1,600, 1,800 and 2,000m. The area is popular with all grades of skier, being as well known for its challenging runs and off-piste skiing as for its very special learning technique for beginners, *ski évolutif*, a method by which you start out on very short skis and gradually progress to longer ones. It is not the only radical innovation for which the

Like most French resorts, Les Arcs is purpose-built with lift systems and ski runs reaching above the tree line.

resort has become famous. Any new ways to enjoy life on skis have always found a pioneering home in Les Arcs: hot dogging, monoskiing, snowboarding, hangliding and parapenting to name but a few. As for international competition, Les Arcs will be the site of the 1992 Olympic course for speed skiing, a sport which has already found a world record-breaking home here for more than a decade. A lift pass for the resort costs £66 at any time throughout the season, and this also allows one day's skiing at either Val d'Isère/Tignes, La Rosière or La Plagne, all of which are located above the Isère valley.

LA PLAGNE

This is another collective resort name, which brings under its wing a number of small ski villages. While much of the architecture is austere the most recent addition, Belle Plagne, has incorporated many traditional styles into its buildings. In all there are 193 km of ski run, making this one of the larger areas, with 95 ski lifts at altitudes up to 3,250 metres. Of the 104 slopes, 7 are black, 34 red, 48 blue and 15 green, all adding up to a lot of scope for every standard. In addition there are 32 kilometres of cross country in the valley of Champagny le Haut, an area reserved exclusively for *langlauf* with tuition available.

MORZINE/AVORIAZ/CHÂTEL

These three French resorts are part of the huge Portes du Soleil ski area, made up of fifteen villages altogether. But where this differs from other multi-resort locations is in its international flavour. Not only because of the people who go there, but because the area itself crosses national boundaries. Of those fifteen villages, seven in fact lie in Switzerland. The overall dimensions of the area are considerable, with 650 kilometres of piste served by 214 lifts and covering all standards. There are at least three nursery slopes per resort, and at the other extreme, between Avoriaz and the Swiss resort of Les Crosets, one of the most testing black runs in the world: the Wall, or to give it its full and more graphic name, 'The white wall of death'. At the top of the Chavanette chair lift you find signs disclaiming any responsibility for personal injury, to mark the beginning of the Wall. Happily you also find a well-used chair lift by which to descend once again, and observe the sheer 300 metre field of monster moguls from a relatively sane viewpoint. In comparison a smooth run down the local World Cup downhill course seems a marginally more attainable goal.

A lift pass for all of these delights costs approximately £55 at low season and rather more than £60 at high. As with the available skiing, so the styles of architecture and the resort facilities serve up plenty of variety, from the futuristic Avoriaz (most definitely purpose-built) to the rather older second-generation resorts of Châtel and Morzine, which are recognized as much for their gourmet excellence as for the challenge of the steep and deep.

FRANCE

	VAL D'ISÈRE/ TIGNES	LES TROIS VALLÉES	LES ARCS	LA PLAGNE	MORZINE/ AVORIAZ/ CHÂTEL
Top Station	3,488m	3,200m	3,226m	3,250m	2,350m
Pisted run	300km	500km	150km	193km	650km
Longest run	13km	8km	10km	15km	6km
Nursery slopes	5	12	4	11	9
Easy runs	25	45	8	13	60
Medium runs	90	155	22	95	80
Difficult runs	10	28	15	7	22
Total No. lifts	102	180	62	100	220
Lift pass (6 days)	£75–85	£67–77	£70–80	£75–80	£55–65
Day nursery	3 months–5 yrs	3–8 yrs	1–6 yrs	3+ yrs	3–14 yrs
Ski nursery	4–12 yrs	3–18 yrs	2–8 yrs	3+ yrs	5–12 yrs
Transfer time from nearest airport	GENEVA 2–3 hrs LYON 5 hrs	LYON 3½ hrs	LYON 4 hrs	LYON 4 hrs	GENEVA 2½ hrs

Rest of Europe

Scandinavia

Scandinavia is of course the home of cross-country skiing, and it is still very much a part of life there. Many major cities have circuits in their parks and suburbs, while in isolated country districts it is still one of the only forms of cheap transport available through the long northern winter, when snow may lie on the ground from October until the end of April. But tourism is also growing, and in particular the Telemark region of Norway (from which came the telemark turn) is now famous for ski touring. There are rest huts and hostels along the better-known routes, though some of the trails are both long and difficult. As for downhill skiing, Alpine style, this has not yet developed to any great extent, because the high mountains needed are here relatively inaccessible. So far the most popular downhill resorts are in southern Norway, at Voss, Gelio and Norefjell – the last being where the 1952 Olympics were held. All these have good ski schools, though holidays there are not cheap.

Germany

There are very few ski resorts in Germany as yet, but Garmisch Partenkirchen, site of the 1936 Olympics, is internationally renowned, not only for its skiing but also for a whole gamut of winter sports activities, especially bobsleigh. The resort is located in the south German region of Bavaria, just across the border from Austria. In addition the Black Forest, in the south-west, specializes in cross-country, under of course its German name of *langlauf*.

A horse and sleigh ride at dusk. The Scandinavians have long made use of skis and sleighs to negotiate snowy terrain.

Eastern Europe

So far only three eastern European countries have developed major resorts: Yugoslavia, Bulgaria and Romania. In Romania skiing is centred on the eastern Carpathians. Generally, my Ski Club of Great Britain sources tell me, the skiing is limited by

Alpine standards, but the ski schools are good. Bulgaria is gaining a reputation for taking British school groups; like other countries in this part of Europe, it has the attraction of being relatively cheap. Yugoslavia of course gained world-wide recognition by staging the Sarajevo Winter Olympics in 1984. As for other countries, the Tatra range of mountains is common to Poland, Czechoslovakia and Hungary, and there are a number of ski resorts in all these countries. So far no international tourism has developed, but with the present rate of change in eastern Europe that lack may not last for long.

Ski runs pass beside thick forests in the mountainous areas of Romania. Here the resort of Poina Brasov can be seen at the end of the cable car run.

| SKI TIPS | Sun and heat can affect you as well as cold. Carry good sunglasses, sun cream and lip salve. |

EASTERN EUROPE

	YUGOSLAVIA KAPAONIK	CZECHOSLOVAKIA SOUTH TATRAS	BULGARIA BOROVETS	ROMANIA POIANA BRADOV
Top Station	1,770m	2,005m	2,399m	1,802m
Pisted run	44km	20km	50km	17km
Longest run	3.5km	3.5km	N/A	N/A
Nursery slopes	1	1	1	4
Easy runs	10	4	7	6
Medium runs	5	10	9	6
Difficult runs	1	6	2	2
Total No. lifts	20	27	14	10
Lift pass (6 days)	£55–65	£13–20	£20–33	£25–35
Day nursery	3–7 yrs	–	2–4 yrs	4–12 yrs
Ski nursery	5+ yrs	–	4–8 yrs	5+ yrs
Transfer time from	NIS	POPRAD	PLOVDIR	BUCHAREST
nearest airport	3 hrs	1½ hrs	2¼ hrs	3 hrs

The Eastern Mediterranean

The largest ski resort in Greece is at Mount Parnassus near Delphi, in the centre of the country. The oldest is on Mount Vermion in the mountains of central Macedonia. Ski touring is also popular, including excursions on Mount Olympus. Further south, there is even skiing in the Mediterranean, on the island of Cyprus. Here you can spend the morning enjoying the snow on their own local Mount Olympus, and the afternoon sunbathing and swimming on the beach an hour's drive away. The Troodos area is the centre of Cypriot skiing, and there are four lifts to choose from.

Andorra

This principality between France and Spain speaks the languages of both its neighbours. It is very cheap and cheerful. There are many British instructors and, as a duty-free area, the après-ski goes with a swing.

Spain

There are a variety of resorts, all of them relatively cheap. Sol y Nieve, near Granada in the Sierra Nevada range, has the distinction of being both the highest resort in Spain (the top lift station is nearly 3,500m high – over 11,000 feet) and the most southerly in Europe. The other Spanish resorts are in the Pyrenees, the largest being Baqueira Beret. Ski hire, instruction, etc., can be haphazard.

Some of the most southerly ski centres in Europe are to be found in Spain. Picturesque old towns lie near to the resorts and provide an excellent opportunity for apres-ski visits.

ANDORRA AND SPAIN

| | ANDORRA | | SPAIN | |
	PAS DE LA CASA	SOLDEU	SOL-Y-NIEVE	FORMIGAL
Top Station	2,530m	2,560m	3,142m	2,350m
Pisted run	55km	52km	50km	30km
Longest run	2km	8.2km	5.5km	3.5km
Nursery slopes	2	3	4	2
Easy runs	18	5	18	16
Medium runs	12	11	11	15
Difficult runs	5	2	5	2
Total No. lifts	27	23	18	16
Lift pass (6 days)	£50–80	£70–80	£53–100	£33–80
Day nursery	3–6 yrs	2½–10 yrs	0–6 yrs	2 months–8 yrs
Ski nursery	–	4–10 yrs	6–12 yrs	–
Transfer time	TOULOUSE	GERONA	GRANADA	ZARAGOZA
from nearest	3½ hrs	5 hrs	1¼ hrs	3½ hrs
airport			MALAGA	
			4 hrs	

Scotland

Despite the bad press which Scotland often suffers because of unreliable snow conditions, there can be excellent skiing. It means that properly lift-served pistes do exist in Britain, and for people in the north of Britain especially, the opportunity for a weekend's skiing is there for the taking. Friends and colleagues say the best way to go about it is to keep the accent on "flexibility". It is definitely a matter of acting on the spur of the moment, they say; just look outside the window, check the weather forecast and go! Conditions are at their best later in the season heading into March, April and even, in some cases, May. Ski schools are excellent, guided by the BASI whose headquarters are at the national ski centre at Aviemore.

AVIEMORE

Lies in the Cairngorm mountains in the Spey Valley between Perth and Inverness. The skiing area and modern ski centre are situated about ten miles away from the village of Aviemore. There are four chair lifts and 11 drag lifts serving the area which comprises about 500 metres of vertical skiing from the summit of Cairngorm at 1,245 metres. Near the top there are nursery slopes as well as easy runs and intermediate pistes. The White Lady chair and tow for the harder slopes with steep runs leave from the Coire Na Ciste car park.

Aonach Mor is the newest ski resort in Britain. Snow may be sporadic but a good weekend's skiing can be had on its slopes.

Cairnwell is adjacent to the main road and is famed as the highest road pass in Britain. The peak there reaches to 3,059ft and holds the famous Tiger Run. There is plenty of hotel and self-catering accommodation in Aviemore and many of the more secluded villages in the area offer bed and breakfast. On the mountain itself a revitalizing cup of tea is rather hard to come by. Realistically speaking, the European variety of mountain cafès and après-ski opportunities are scarce in Scotland, but then the Scottish experience is unique unto itself and has never tried to emulate the Alps.

LECHT AND GLENSHEE
To the north of Aviemore is the very small area of Lecht which lies between Grantown and Braemar. Still in the Cairngorms to the south is Glenshee which is between Braemar and Perth. New lifts and runs have been added here in recent years and skiing starts at the roadside car park.

GLENCOE
In the Western Highlands are both the oldest and newest ski areas, known collectively as Lochaber. Glencoe has been recognized as a long weekend destination for many years but now it is joined by Aonach Mor, which lies above the town of Fort William.

AONACH MOR
The construction of this ski area was completed in just over a year and opened in December 1989. It has been created on Britain's eighth highest mountain and is overshadowed by the highest, Ben Nevis. From outside Fort William the first gondola of its kind in Britain takes skiers from the sea level car park to 650 metres. The nursery and beginners' slopes are located around the gondola station, where the mountain restaurant, the Snow Goose, is situated. The rest of the lower area is intermediate territory and access is via a quad chair. On the highest reaches are the steeper slopes for more advanced skiers. In all there are seven lifts, both tow and chair.

Fort William is 4 ½ miles away and has more than 9,000 tourist beds available. Glasgow is about a hundred miles to the south.

North America

North America is now attracting increasing attention as an alternative to the Alps – exchange rates permitting! British interest in transatlantic skiing destinations stems in part from the erratic snow conditions experienced throughout the Alps in the last couple of years, and also from cheaper US flights. Of course, air travel across the Atlantic cannot match charter-flight prices from Britain to the European continent, so an American holiday will inevitably cost more than its European equivalent. Nevertheless more tour operators than ever before are now finding it worthwhile to offer destinations in the USA. Many resorts there are certainly famed throughout the skiing world for their powder snow; and, even more to the point, for their guarantee of good conditions, since "snow making" and the production of artificial snow are matters of high expertise over there. As a result the season in the Rockies and Colorado is guaranteed to run from the end of November (the American holiday of Thanksgiving is the traditional start) right through to late April or early May.

Sun Valley, Idaho, is recognized as the first purpose-built resort in the USA, dating back to 1934. Many of the resorts, however, possess a historical link with America's pioneering past. Most started out in the 1800s as mining centres or ranching towns, and saw decay and desolation before the ski business regenerated them. Breckenridge in Colorado, for instance, was officially designated a ghost town in the 1950s.

But whether purpose-built or rejuvenated settlement, American ski resorts show many differences from Europe both on and off the pistes (or trails as the Americans call them). Primarily the

Silver birch and aspen trees abound in Beaver Creek, where you can step out of your log cabin into freshly fallen snow.

accent is on customer service. The trails are manicured and groomed to phenomenal standards. Some may say it is too much, since throughout a day's skiing on easy and intermediate runs you will rarely face even the hint of a mogul bump. Trails also tend to be wide (no dangerous bottlenecks) and landscaped through forests. (The Americans have a real bonus in the form of a tree line which extends to 11,000 feet; much higher than Europe where the trees disappear at about 7,000 feet). The runs tend to be a lot shorter than in Europe, but the lift facilities are efficient and quick so you can be back skiing much sooner. There are very few drag lifts, so even over the shortest distances you usually travel in comfort in either gondolas or chair lifts – and padded ones at that! Lift queues are a rarity, lift attendants will actually smile and pass the time of day, and there is probably even a box of tissues in the lift line to accommodate the slightest sniffle. Lift passes are expensive at perhaps $20 a day, but the resorts and British package companies do discount prices for a one or two week stay.

The major reason for expensive lift tickets and the squeaky-clean state of the trails is the threat of litigation. Americans will sue anyone for negligence, and a relatively robust occupation like skiing is a gold mine for lawyers and successful plaintiffs alike. There are of course expert skiing runs and powder bowls served by lifts, but they are kept completely separate from the tourist trails. The idea of off-piste skiing does not exist. If ski patrols see a skier outside the clearly marked resort boundaries they have the power to fine and perhaps imprison the offender. One great advantage of America's "Sue-City" nervousness is the condition of hire equipment. It has to be of a very high standard, since the costs of making a mistake are very expensive. Make sure, therefore, that as a holiday maker you too are adequately insured for a trip to the USA.

SKI TIPS	Fear – become aware of your own inner tension. It is a natural feeling in any physical activity and is often useful. But sometimes positive arousal is replaced by negative fear. In skiing, fear comes from the physical threat of falling; from the psychological effect of wondering what other people think we look like, and from fear of the unknown. It is quite natural to feel fear when faced with terrain we are not used to, or with the challenge of mastering a difficult technique. By learning to control our emotions we will allow our peak performance to become more accessible.

Many American resorts are very high. The resort base may start at 8,000 or 9,000 feet and rise up to 11,500 feet or more, so be careful to consider the effects of altitude. It is important to take it easy for the first couple of days (especially when it comes on top of jet lag). A common sight by the side of a trail are ski patrols and ski stewardesses dispensing whiffs of oxygen from the first aid kits; or, as in one case I saw, hot chocolate from a customized back pack! Altitude also has an effect on alcohol tolerance. I am told one drink at 9,000 feet is the same as three at sea level. It's another cost saving anyway!

A quad chair lift complete with back canopy for extra comfort – all part of the luxury of an American holiday.

On the subject of cost, it does not come as a surprise in the free-marketing USA that the best bargains in lift tickets can often be found at the competing petrol stations and grocery stores in the foothills around the resorts. Tuition is, unfortunately, expensive; but it is in English – with a big slice of all-American cheerleading "get up and go". As for the resorts themselves, the standards of decor and service are simply very high indeed, whether you are talking of hotels, chalets or restaurants. Something uniquely American is the condominium or "condo". Its counterpart in Europe is the apartment; at least, in that both are bought or rented as self-catering living accommodation. There however the similarity ends, because the condo is the ultimate in fittings and furnishings. All the details which would be luxurious extras in the European equivalent are likely to be standard in the USA: e.g. microwaves, dishwashers, even hot tubs (outdoor jacuzzis). The last of these will either be shared by a block of condos, or in the more élite properties provided as a blissful private facility. In addition, even though condos are let on a self-catering basis, it is quite common to have maid service as standard in the price. The other important difference (apart from a log fire!) is the space given to bedrooms and living quarters. British people I have met, who have purchased condos in Colorado, say that costwise you can get in dollars what you would talk about in pounds in Britain. Another refreshing aspect of American skiing is the value for money when it comes to food and drink. Even in a mountain restaurant prices are rarely distorted, and the portions are sizeable to say the least.

NEW ENGLAND

	KILLINGTON
Top Station	1,293m/4,241ft
Pisted run	74km/46¼ miles
Longest run	18km/11¼ miles
Nursery slopes	7
Easy runs	51
Medium runs	25
Difficult runs	41
Total No. lifts	18
Lift pass (6 days)	£110–120
Day nursery	–
Ski nursery	2–8 yrs
Transfer time from	BOSTON
nearest airport	3 hrs

CANADA

	BANFF
Top Station	2,730m/8,954ft
Pisted run	N/A
Longest run	8km/5 miles
Nursery slopes	3
Easy runs	2
Medium runs	2
Difficult runs	2
Total No. lifts	N/A
Lift pass (6 days)	£95–135
Day nursery	–
Ski nursery	–
Transfer time from	CALGARY
nearest airport	2½ hrs

Areas

There are three main ski-resort areas in North America. In the east is New England, and the neighbouring mountain areas of the northern Appalachians and the Canadian Laurentians. Most famous here is the New York State resort of Lake Placid, which has twice been home to the Winter Olympics. I have heard New England skiing described as having a "stark" quality. It's said that one west-coast skier, coming east for the first time, hoped to impress his host by saying that in Colorado he was used to deep powder up to his elbows. The host replied that in New England he would enjoy a rather different experience, with frozen granular up to his edges. Even New England cynicism is relative though, since like all Americans they expect so much from their ski conditions, and their snow-making sophistication ensures open pistes. New England also has a charm all of its own, from the Green Mountains of Vermont through the White Mountains of New Hampshire to the Longfellow range of Maine. Stowe in Vermont, for example, has many wood-built lodges, and a surprisingly genuine sense of history for a relatively young country.

These are the lowest-lying of North American resorts, reaching to about 1,800 metres, 6,000 feet. Sugarloaf in Maine is one of the most easterly, and recently added to its notoriety by being the launchpad for Richard Branson's balloon crossing of the Atlantic. "The Loaf", as it is known by locals, can seem an enigma even by American standards. Not only does it provide all the necessities of the ultimate consumer society, with thirteen restaurants and an $8,000,000 hotel (along of course with such resort essentials as banks, laundromat and video rental store). It also finds time to pay annual tribute to an endangered species each December, when Sugar Loaf hosts Yellow-Nosed Vole Day... The geography of the place can take some acclimatization too, with tongue twisters like Mooselookmeguntic and Matawamkeag, plus 70 trails through 440 acres of "skiable terrain", 80 per cent of which is supplemented by snow-making from early November to early May.

Like a spotlight in a theatre you can either spread your attention over large areas or pin-point one spot. In mogul fields, for example, narrow your concentration and pick the best places to turn before you set off. Concentrate on the soft snow that collects on the uphill side of a mogul bump instead of on the icy down-side of the bump, which your skis should not need to touch.

SKI TIPS

In the west, and north of the US-Canadian border, are the northern Rockies, where peaks reach anything up to 3,700 metres, 12,000 feet. Here the famous resorts include the Banff ski area and Whistler Mountain, which is one of the World Cup venues for downhill races. But this region has also specialized in the development of heli-skiing to remote areas of untouched snow, opening up such distant-sounding settings as the Bugaboo, Cariboo and Monashee Mountains. One other destination which is seriously north by anyone's compass bearing is Anchorage, Alaska, and the Alyeska ski area. The mountain only rises to 3,939 feet, but it is so far north that snow is usually guaranteed; though the hours of daylight are a bit limited in the middle of winter!

Finally there are the Rockies of the USA proper. Here the peaks are the highest in North America, and a ski-resort top station may rise to 4,300 metres, 14,000 feet. This is the place for powder snow – and for memories of pioneering days. You can still tell the resorts with ranching origins because the main street was built wide, to herd cattle to the rail-head. In mining towns the main throughfares were kept narrow, no doubt for the equally practical reason of minimizing the distance between bars. Many of the names in fact still conjur up a frontier past. There are Crested Butte and Purgatory in Colorado, Jackson Hole in Wyoming, Snowbird in Utah; while the California-Nevada border boasts the Lake Tahoe ski area, which includes the resorts of Heavenly Valley and Squaw Valley.

In most resorts this past is simply history of course. For example, the old mining town of Teluhride was once the scene of Butch Cassidy's first illicit bank withdrawal; but these days it is only the skiing which is wild. However the old ways are still strong sometimes, as at Steamboat Springs, which got its name not from any ferries which somehow found their way to the mountains, but from the sound the local spring water made as it came out of the ground. Here every year the summer ranching town hosts a winter cowboy skiing rodeo, at which skiing ability is of little consequence compared with important things like the size of your stetson and the length of your lassoo. But then, like many of the most famous Rockies' resorts, Steamboat is in Colorado, where there is a certain other centre at which skiing sometimes matters less than style.

ASPEN

Even though the sun may go down on a skiing day, Aspen is one of those places that seem just as bright by night. At Christmas time one suspects that Hollywood and New York suffer a serious celebrity drain, as the streets and ski slopes of Aspen become an irresistible draw. Though people who come to Aspen are not the type who have to show off their wealth. All you need is a smart pair of jeans and your own executive Leah jet. There are more than a hundred restaurants and night spots patronized by the well-heeled. The town centre is traffic free, if you discount the odd reindeer or llama ride. Window shopping is about all mere mortals can indulge in, without taking out an extra mortgage.

Float through the snow-capped trees on chair lifts over Aspen, Colorado.

Aspen is actually four mountains: Aspen mountain itself is served by the $17,000,000 Silver Queen gondola, elevating skiers 3,267 feet from base level to the top. The longest run is three miles, and including the Buttermilk mountain there are 402 acres of groomed trails. There is also Snowmass, which has become a resort in its own right, with 1,500 acres of tree-lined trails and 17 lifts. While these three mountains are run by the Aspen corporation, there is also another, privately owned mountain called Aspen Highland. Multi-day lift tickets are, however, interchangeable.

Despite the wealth around, or more probably because of it, there are certain idiosyncrasies which are truly Aspen. The staff at the local McDonalds burger bar are reputed to be the best paid in the whole of the company's world-wide chain. There is a rugby union pitch in the heart of the town and a mere twenty yards from the skiing, the land of which, if it were to be developed, would be worth many millions of dollars. Yet community solidarity and many local statutes decree that its particular function will never change. (As a finishing touch to the stamp of tradition, the rugby posts have been made out of the indigenous aspen trees from which the town gets its name.) One hotel which has opened in the 1990 season (built of course to the three-storey town maximum) is the Little Nell, of particular interest to skiers because it has its own ski concièrge. As part of a very expensive stay you can ski to the hotel door and leave your skis and boots with a special porter. He then attaches a personalized pair of tubes to your boots to blow room-temperature air gently through them overnight, while waxing and servicing your skis. As a final touch, when you come to put your boots on in the morning, awaiting you are freshly brewed coffee and cakes.

VAIL/BEAVER CREEK

Vail it seems, knows what it has got and flaunts it. In just twenty-five years the town has grown into one of the best-known ski resorts in the world. There have been two unusual agents in this development: the Indians and the US army. The original settlers in the Gore Valley were the Ute Indians, and after the white man's final intrusion their last act was to set fire to thousands of acres of timberland. The result was the now-famous Vail powder Back Bowls. Originally there were two, consisting of 800 acres and named Sun Up and Sun Down. In 1988 another 1,881 acres were added with China, Siberia, Teacup and Mongolia bowls, and the acreage is now up to 4,000 acres as of 1990. The second important factor was, as mentioned, the US army, which trained its Tenth Mountain Division in the Vail area during the Second World War. After the war many of those in the Division wanted to keep up their newly learnt skiing skills, and even now in the vast wilderness between Vail and Aspen the skiing huts of the Tenth Mountain Division are regularly visited by cross-country and ski-touring groups.

Since it also hosted the 1989 World Alpine Ski Championships (the only American resort apart from Aspen to have received this honour) it might seem so far that Vail is only for the mad or expert or both. Nothing could be further from the truth, with 120 groomed trails of every type on more than 1,000 acres, and a massive children's centre at the recently opened Golden Peak base. Like any good American resort they are also very quick to bombard you with superlatives. For instance there are more high-speed detachable quad lifts at the resort than any other in the world!

American resorts pride themselves on being able to offer year-round entertainment; Vail also provides fishing in beautiful surroundings in the warmer months.

Meanwhile Beaver Creek, once a mere satellite of Vail, has grown up to become a substantial partner. Much of the newly developed area is made up of privately owned houses for the truly rich and famous, from Hollywood stars to ex-Presidents. The Village Plaza Hotel complexes are sumptuous, with some of the most prestigious fine art galleries sharing partition walls with ski rental shops. Like Vail the resort rises from a base level of about 8,000 feet up to 11,500 feet, and in its own right Beaver Creek has 49 runs over 800 acres.

Ironically Vail and Beaver Creek look less than their best seen from their major transport artery. The Interstate 70 is Colorado's primary motorway, cutting east-west through the State, and the resorts have been squeezed between the mountains and the four-lane motorway in a long strip development stretching more than five miles. The big plus of course is the ease of access from Denver, which is only 90 miles to the west via roads which do not wind round hairpin Alpine-style bends. But inside the resorts, in any case, it is a very different story. Despite the road's proximity the exhaust fumes and traffic noise simply vanish; and in their place is an amazing concatenation of architectural styles, with passing cosmopolitan references to Tyrolian hostelries, London pubs and Japanese sushi bars.

SUMMIT COUNTY
This is the group name for some of the best skiing areas in Colorado: Breckenridge, Copper Mountain, Keystone and Arapahoe Basin. They lie together no more than 75 miles from Denver (again on the Interstate 70). Each resort has a very distinctive flavour, yet they are all within twenty minutes' drive of each other with free bus service connections too. There is an international Ski the Summit pass for all the areas, covering eight mountain peaks, 55 lifts, over 250 trails and nearly 4,000 acres of skiable terrain.

Breckenridge is real mining country. The largest single gold nugget ever found, weighing more than 13 pounds, was mined here in the 1860s. By the Second World War surveyors had forgotten to put what was left of post-gold rush Breckenridge on the maps. But in 1961 the Breckenridge Ski Area was opened, and now they are mining a rich seam of "white gold" as the resort goes from strength to strength. It provides relatively good value compared with glitzy Vail and is becoming a major centre for British tour operators. It has not however lost its nineteenth-century charm, with more than a hundred original or part-original buildings still in existence, along with many more shops, galleries, restaurants and boutiques. The resort comprises three interconnecting mountains. Peaks Eight and Nine have the easy and intermediate trails, while the most difficult runs (about 50 per cent of the skiing) are concentrated on Peak Ten and the Back Bowls of Peak Eight.

Copper Mountain (which as the name suggests also has a mining history) calls itself the "skier's mountain". It has certainly won many American awards for layout, with the terrain dividing naturally into advanced (35 per cent), intermediate (40 per cent) and beginner (25 per cent) areas, above a purpose-built resort with accommodation, restaurants and ski lifts all within walking distance.

Keystone is famous for its 13 ½ hour ski day. As daylight fades so the floodlights come on: all 300 high-pressure sodium lights, illuminating 200 acres and 13 runs. The effect is a whole mountain which from the distance looks like white molten lava. Skiing at Keystone is available on three faces and two mountains. Like every good "planned" American resort the front face at Keystone is carefully apportioned, 65 per cent intermediate, 20 per cent beginner, while advanced skiing makes up about 78 per cent of the adjacent North Peak. Finally, Arapahoe Basin is located a few miles from Keystone Village. With a summit at 12,450 feet, perched on top of the North American continental divide, it is one of the highest skiing areas in the USA and stays open until June.

A ride along tree-lined passes in the old mining town of Breckenridge; a century ago, gold would have been transported in these sledges.

The basic swing links the snowplough with the parallel skid. The turn is initiated using the snowplough, then when ready the inside ski is turned parallel to create a controlled skid.

SKIING FROM SALT LAKE CITY

While Denver is the main transport centre serving Colorado's ski areas, another airport hub is Salt Lake City which opens up both Utah and Wyoming. There are eight major ski resorts on the cities' doorstep (within an hour's drive). Salt Lake City is fast becoming a ski destination in its own right with thousands of skiers staying there and travelling each day to the best snow at Alta, Brighton, Deer Valley, Park West, Snowbasin, Snowbird, Solitude or Park City.

Park City, an old silver mining town, is Utah's largest ski area with 62 pisted runs and 2,200 acres of ski area, 650 acres of which is off-piste bowl skiing. If you are not with a charter company, nor hiring a car there are regular bus services from the airport. Like many American resorts, Park City is well planned with areas especially designated for beginners, intermediates and experts. The lift capacity includes 7 double chair lifts, 5 triple chair lifts, one high speed quad and a four-seater gondola. Lift passes cost about $35 per day. Ski school is an integral part of American ski resorts; an all-day group ski school lesson for 7-10 people will cost about $33 for 4 hours' teaching.

COLORADO

	ASPEN	VAIL	BRECKENRIDGE
Top Station	3,418m/11,211ft	3,429m/11,247ft	3,734m/12,247ft
Pisted run	197km/123 miles	90km/56 miles	80km/50 miles
Longest run	6km/3¾ miles	7km/4¼ miles	2km/1¼ miles
Nursery slopes	23	2	2
Easy runs	49	24	31
Medium runs	100	27	32
Difficult runs	69	24	47
Total No. lifts	40	18	14
Lift pass (6 days)	£80–120	£80–100	£70–100
Day nursery	–	2–6 yrs	0–3 yrs
Ski nursery	3+ yrs	2½–12 yrs	3–6 yrs
Transfer time from nearest airport	ASPEN 1 hr	DENVER 2½ hrs	DENVER 2 hrs

Exotic Locations

Exotic locations range considerably in price and distance. Morocco, for instance, is no more difficult to reach by air than Austria or Switzerland, and winter skiing holidays there offer good value together with the chance to experience a little of a very different culture. At the other extreme, Japan is half a world away, and Japanese prices high enough to test the toughest credit card. Then there are the destinations south of the equator. No less expensive, because of the distances involved; but, since their seasons run from about May to October, very tempting to those who are longing for a sight of snow when others around them are content with sun and sand. One other point in their favour is the fair likelihood of good tuition, since it is not only ski holidaymakers who migrate south during the "off" season, but also many of the best instructors.

Japan

Most of the ski resorts in Japan are located on dormant or extinct volcanoes. There are hundreds of resorts in the country, but all the same they do become crowded, and the piste runs are generally shorter than their Alpine equivalents. The Japanese obsession with the sport stems from the work of an Austrian, Theodore von Lech, who brought the concept of skiing to the Far East in the early part of this century. The season is approximately the same as the European one, December to April. The biggest resort is Shiga Heights, near Nagaro in the centre of Japan, comprising over twenty separate ski areas and more than eighty lifts. Some of the tour operators warn in their brochures that it is worth taking your own ski boots, because the average Japanese foot is relatively small and therefore any boot hire usually has to be done by prior arrangement.

India

The British have been skiing in India for many years, but only recently has foreign tourism developed with an international clientele available who are prepared to pay for an alternative ski experience. Because of the remoteness of the ski areas the establishment of heli-skiing has also made a difference. The main centre is at Gulmarg in Kashmir, where there are now eleven hotels and many more pensions. The resort provides pisted skiing along with cross-country trails, and snow falls between November and May. A typical package for eleven nights, combining five days at the Gulmarg ski resort with six in Delhi and Jaipur, and including Indian domestic flights as well as the long-haul return, would cost between £870 and £1,000.

Australia

This country has had a longer association with skiing than most, since immigrant Norwegians formed the first Australian ski club in the middle of the nineteenth century. The Snowy Mountains of New South Wales, part of the Australian Alpine chain, have the highest resorts and the most consistent snow cover. (However some of the placenames, like Perisher Valley, leave you in no doubt about former hard times.) Mount Buller in Victoria is the largest ski resort in the country. This state is also recognized for its cross-country skiing and ski touring. I am told that the Australian ski season begins on the Queen's birthday (with or without snow) in June and ends in September.

New Zealand

The holiday pamphlets will tell you that here there is guaranteed snow, low prices at the resorts, few crowds and a tremendous variety of terrain and types of skiing. The only problem is, New Zealand is 1,200 miles further even than Australia and in all about 12,000 miles by air from the UK, with a minimum flying time of over twenty-three hours and prices to match. The season lasts between June and October, and much of the best skiing in New Zealand is only accessible by air, so heli-skiing is well developed. There are more than twenty ski centres, mostly on South Island where the largest resorts include Coronet Peak near Queenstown, Mount Cook National Park and Mount Hutt. North Island skiing is characterized by the use of volcanic mountains. There is skiing around Mount Ruapehu to the south, and to the west around Mount Egmont.

South America

As with many of these distant destinations, the average skier will never be able to enjoy the exotic atmosphere of a South American holiday. But there are those with the wage packet to afford it, and the will to do something different. One suitably different choice of destination might be Punta Arenas in Chile, which has the distinction of being the most southerly ski resort in the world. Skiing is in fact quite well established in Chile, which has a World Alpine Championship to its name. Argentina has also profited from the World Cup circuit, and has well-known resorts on her side of the Andes at San Carlos de Bariloche and Las Lenas. But if skiing at the other end of the world is a pleasant dream, beware the cost of the reality. A ten-day package holiday in San Carlos costs over £700 for half board in a twin room; and while that covers unlimited use of the ski lifts, it does not include often hefty high-season supplements, *nor* the cost of the plane flight there and back.

Do-It-Yourself Transport

Every year thousands more decide to go to the Continent on a do-it-yourself trip to Europe's ski resorts, either by car, bus, train, or a combination of these (including perhaps a flight to one of Europe's international airports).

Of course it is difficult to beat the value of the standard package holiday, which includes transport. But there are also packages without transport, offered by the resorts themselves through their tourist offices or by hotel chains, and these are what many DIY travellers choose. Known as *forfaits* (the French term), they may include accommodation and board, lift pass, ski-school fees, perhaps even ski and boot hire. Everything in fact except transport to the resort; and they can be very good value, especially at the start and end of the season.

GOING BY CAR

Most of those committed enough to take their own car on a skiing holiday will also have skis to take with them. You can hire or buy a ski box to fit on top of the car roof. Rental charges, on AA figures, are £4 per day, while to buy one, depending on the size, works out between £200 and £400. The larger ones are designed to take four complete sets of ski gear including ski clothes and boots.

But whether you will be carrying skis or not, for all those taking cars abroad there are a number of car accessories which are requirements on the Continent which are not compulsory in the UK. These are: a warning triangle; spare bulbs; a first-aid kit (compulsory in Austria); and a fire extinguisher (compulsory in Greece). The AA hire out an emergency pack which contains all these extras and many more at £1.25 a day. Green card insurance is also a must. Even if you have fully comprehensive insurance in the UK, it automatically drops to third-party level without the back-up of a green card. (Incidentally, make sure that all documents, including passport, driving licence, insurance and breakdown details, are always easily accessible.) Finally, remember that seat belts are compulsory in many countries, and that some do not allow children to travel in the front seat.

Snow-chains are essential for anyone driving in the mountains. Whether you buy or hire, do practise fitting them a few times, on the drive or in the garage; because, from bitter experience, it is far more difficult when it comes to doing it for real on a mountain road! Make the decision to put chains on the tyres when you are still in control and can park by the side of the road in a clearly visible spot.

Give yourself extra freedom by going by car – but do make sure you have all the correct equipment for a trouble-free holiday.

Coming from left-hand drive Britain to right-hand Europe, remember to convert headlamps. The legal requirement is to cover over that part of the headlamp which would deflect a UK headlamp beam to the left and directly into oncoming traffic. Templates for every type of left-hand drive vehicle can be purchased; just cut out the required sticky-backed shape for your headlamps. In France it is a courtesy to paint lamps with a yellow lacquer. This too can be purchased in Britain and it does scrub off eventually.

Make sure you have anti-freeze and de-icing washer liquid, and in sufficient quantities to cope with very low temperatures. Keep a small shovel easily accessible – however fully laden the car.

Remember the GB sticker for the back. When parking your car be certain to lift up the wipers so they do not freeze to the windscreen. The AA suggest that it is worth finding a flat stretch to park the car (especially if it will be there for some time). This means the handbrake is not required and thereby eliminates the danger of the cable freezing in the "on" position. As an extra precaution leave the car in reverse or in first gear. If the car is stationary for some while make time to clear away the build-up of snow around it after a fall. It could be quite a task if you leave it until the end of the week! Leave the snow over the windows, however, because it acts as an insulator so that solid ice (which can take some shifting) cannot form.

Have enough local currency ready for tolls, in France, Italy, Spain, Yugoslavia and Austria. Non-toll roads will take much longer, but do save the expense of course. In Switzerland foreign motorists should display a toll disc. These can be purchased in Britain from the Swiss Tourist Office, the AA and RAC.

What with petrol, insurance, extra equipment, road tolls, and meals on the way, the expenses of going by car certainly mount up, and once you add in other factors such as the time and effort involved, the danger of breakdown, accident or delay (especially with winter road conditions), and the state of tiredness you may arrive in, most people decide it is not for them. But if the thought of the above is daunting, yet you would still like to have the flexibility to change locations once you get to the mountains, then there are a couple of solutions. One is motorail: services from Paris run to St Gervais, Moutiers, Grenoble and Nice, so giving access to the whole breadth of the French Alps, and there is also a link to the Pyrenees via Narbonne and Tarbes. The other option is a fly-drive package, which is offered by a number of airlines in conjunction with major car rental companies like Budget and Hertz. Of course, if you simply want some mobility around a fixed base, perhaps so you can do some sight-seeing as well as skiing, there is nothing to stop you going on a regular package holiday but hiring a car for day trips.

Nose/feet turns. For a short-radius turn, the skis are turned more quickly by a pivoting action of the legs. Aid the movement with a firm pole plant at the start of the turn. Develop upper/lower body separation. Think of nose/feet turns. The nose follows the direction of travel and the feet turn across this direction.

SKI TIPS

GOING BY RAIL, COACH OR AIR

One of the most recent innovations by an enterprising tour operator is the disco train. A chance to flex the leg muscles for a whole twenty hours! Acclimatization more for après-ski perhaps than for the daylight downhill activities. The rail to ski-resort journey, however, has a long tradition (even longer than a remixed disco beat), especially to the older resorts. From Calais there are locations with direct links, including the Austrian resorts of St Anton and Badgastein which are over 20 hours away. Swiss St Moritz is one change away, so too is Davos and Zermatt. Klosters is two changes and 19 hours away. The French high speed train, the TGV, will quickly sweep skiers from Paris to the south and east. From Bourg St Maurice, a railway junction grown into a Tarentaise town, the resorts of Les Arcs, Val d'Isère and Tignes are all within striking distance. La Plagne is close by, serviced by the town of Aime. To the north Chamonix is one change away, after the cross-channel crossing.

There is also the international express coach service which runs via Grenoble, Chambéry, Annecy and Geneva, taking twenty-two hours. Finally there is do-it-yourself air travel (as opposed to buying a package). Many major international airports specialize in "processing" skiers on their way to the slopes: Munich, Salzburg, Lyons, Milan, Turin, Nice, Berne, Zurich, and of course Geneva. All have public transport to the resorts; in fact at Geneva you can push your luggage trolley through customs, down the escalator and straight onto the train platform, in a welcoming sample of customary Swiss efficiency.

CHAPTER FOUR

Ways to Ski

There are many ways to ski, and over the years for pleasure and competition the ingenious have had a go at just about everything.

Alpine Racing

Have you ever suspected that all racers were born without a safety catch in their heads? They will tell you there is nothing to it.

An expert skier's signature in the snow – shown here in the perfect curves of an off-piste run.

Simply hurl yourself down the steepest mountain the organizers can find, negotiate the odd bend or two, and do it a mere one-hundredth of a second quicker than anyone else.

For its sheer exhilaration and bravery, Alpine skiing has turned itself into one of the most talked about sports in the international calender. What is more, this circus of supreme athletic talent rolls into towns throughout the Alps, the Americas and Japan every year. Though you may not get the best view of a race by being there, it really is worth going to see an Alpine meeting just once, if only to make your television viewing come alive. The sound of a racer flying down a sheer icy slope is like a passing train, and along with the sense of speed it is a never-to-be-forgotten experience.

Surprisingly it was the British who were the first to attempt the feat, at Crans Montana in 1911, much to the incredulity of their Swiss hosts. Nowadays the World Cup series, which was introduced in 1967, covers all the Alpine disciplines at the highest level: downhill, slalom, giant slalom, and, since 1983, super-giant slalom (super-G). There are about thirty World Cup meetings around the world in the course of a year, and the cumulative results give not only champions in each discipline but also an overall Champion of Champions for the year. Every two years there is a World Championship, and every four years of course the Olympic Games.

The first Winter Olympics to include Alpine events were staged in 1936, and legendary performances have been building up ever since. Some of the great names, both men and women, include Jean-Claude Killy of France; Toni Sailer, Karl Schranz, Franz Klammer and Anne-Marie Moser-Pröll from Austria; the Swede Ingemar Stenmark; Rosi Mittermaier, the West German; Marc Girardelli, an Austrian who skis for Luxembourg; and a clutch of Swiss stars including Pirmin Zurbriggen, Erica Hess, Maria Walliser and Michela Figini.

DOWNHILL
In the downhill nowadays speeds of 80 mph and more are common, routes are strictly defined and the piste is perfectly manicured for the race. Safety has become an important element in course design, while for skiers to attain such speeds and be competitive involves year-round application to their sport. In the summer months time will be spent building up basic stamina and strength, both in the gym and pounding out the miles on the road. Glacier skiing during the summer can never replicate the gradient and conditions of a World Cup race, but preparation time here is nevertheless crucial for improving technique, while

there is always the need to test new skis. Though a top racer may have many pairs of seemingly identical skis supplied by a manufacturer, carefully controlled time trials have proved that a favoured "quick" pair will always come to light. If not, it is probably time to change sponsors!

The World Cup tour embraces so many continents now, that racing will begin perhaps in October and run through to the end of February. This makes stamina, and attention to detail at the race venue, ever more important. Not just physical fitness and diet but also psychological and mental qualities come into play. When one-hundredth of a second marks the difference between winner and runner-up, then nothing can be left to chance. Each team will inspect every foot of the course, which may be perhaps four kilometres long with a descent of up to 1,000 metres, just to find the optimum route. Unlike other Alpine disciplines, downhill competitors are compelled to practise on the actual course in the days preceding the race. Training runs (they are usually allowed three) are videoed and timed to get a feel of the conditions and to perfect technique – as well as to take a look at how the opposition are doing too.

The best courses test a range of different skills; for example, racers' bravery when confronted with several jumps into thin air. Here the art is to "suck" the jump by pushing weight and hands forward. Every racer fears that a jump initiated with his bodyweight too far back will allow the wind to catch under the ski tips, flipping him onto his back. Not surprisingly it is the most common fall among downhillers. Another danger area is compressions: concave features, like the bottom of a roller coaster, where a racer may experience forces of three or four Gs. A downhiller's ability to "glide" will be tested over long straights as he maintains a crouched tuck position, while the quality of his turns lies in the precision with which they are achieved. The headlong rush down the mountain may look impressive, but it is on the turns especially that the momentum of a run is built or destroyed.

SLALOM

Slalom events were again a British invention, introduced in the 1920s as a test of a skier's ability to manoeuvre round obstacles, such as trees – and, in those pre-lift days, as a form of competition that didn't involve the exhaustion of trudging to the top of a downhill piste! As these events gained in popularity they split into varying forms: slalom, giant slalom and, as the most recent addition, super giant, generally known as super-G.

Tomba, the Italian world champion and gold medalist, demonstrates his skill on the giant slalom course.

SLALOM

The present-day slalom course certainly bears little relationship to any traditional art of negotiating 30-foot Christmas trees. Nowadays competitors are faced with poles marking between 55 and 75 gates on a men's course, 45 and 60 on a women's, and requiring more than a turn a second.

The overall course has a vertical drop of up to 220 metres for the men, 180 metres for women, and must include certain specified layouts of gate. In 1982 "rapid" poles, which have a universal spring-loaded joint at snow level, replaced the traditional poles of bamboo, and since their introduction slalom experts have developed a style more akin to a world boxing champ, as they take the closest possible line through the gates. With helmet and heavy padding on hands and limbs, the slalom skier now explodes through the poles, knocking it aside with an arm or leg while making sure that his or her skis travel just that vital fraction to the assigned side of the gate.

Success or failure is measured literally in inches, and though courses are relatively short they can be icy, which does not simplify matters for the competitors as they bob and swerve their way through the alternating blue and red gates. A World Cup race is decided over two runs, over two courses set out alongside each other. Perhaps a hundred will enter the race but only the top thirty make it into the second round, with the winner being the quickest over both runs.

GIANT SLALOM This was introduced just before the Second World War, in part as a way of bringing Alpine racing to venues without the length of run for a full downhill course. It first qualified as an Olympic event in 1952, and many experts reckon it is the most demanding of the Alpine disciplines, both physically and in terms of technical accuracy. Gates are far wider than in slalom, and further apart, while courses are longer and their drops greater (up to 400 metres for men, 350 metres for women). So in effect the event is between normal slalom and downhill in character. Runs typically take one to one and a half minutes, and again events involve two runs over different courses, though in this case both legs can take place down the same piste as long as the gates are repositioned. Technique for the giant slalom places a high premium on crouched, flowing turns.

SUPER-GIANT SLALOM This is a relatively new event, which only reached World Championship status in 1987. Alpine racing had become increasingly specialized, with downhill racers seldom succeeding in slalom or giant slalom events and vice versa. So super-G was introduced with the idea of evening up the balance between speed and technical events, and giving the pure speed men a more equal chance of scoring points towards the overall Champion of Champions title. Super-G competitors wear the same kit as downhill racers: protective helmets and close-fitting aerodynamic suits. Decided over one run, the event is a smaller version of a downhill in length – combining the precision of a winding course, marked by gates, with speeds of up to 50 mph.

FREESTYLE SKIING

Freestyle is different: a sport born to push back the frontiers of skiing with a snowstorm of thrills! When it began, in the 1960s, it was called hot-dogging: an American form of lunacy where anything went, and frequently did. But since then it has grown into the only form of competition skiing which is not won on minimum time or maximum distance but on scores for skill and aesthetics. There are three disciplines: the explosive power of the moguls, the gymnastic courage of the aerials, and the artistry of the ballet. Skiers may specialize in one of them, or compete for the combined title. Freestyle as a competitive event was finally recognized by the International Ski Federation only in 1981, but since then it has been a demonstration event in the 1988 Calgary Olympics, and full status will be given to some of the freestyle elements for 1992.

MOGULS Skiing at full tilt down a fieldful of bumps: if speed skiing and downhill racing seem to be for near-lunatics, you should take a careful look at what the mogul specialists get up to!

But what may appear barely under control is really the product of superb skill and balance; the knees and hips acting as shock absorbers, while the body, always pointing down the fall line, is passive and steady, expending as little energy as possible. Experts will tell you that a good mogul skier's head seems to remain at a constant height, despite his legs working like pistons over the undulations. At competition level the quality of balance, turns and contact with the snow are all scored by the panel of judges, along with "air" or jumps. The last are for the experts only, but in a competition run a skier can attempt two jumps, and they can be high point scorers if they are landed properly.

If you feel that you have mastered all there is to learn about skiing, think again and try some ballet movements on snow!

AERIALS A word of warning: any newcomer to this next event should only try it under careful and expert supervision. But if it is far too dangerous for ignorant experiment, it is certainly well worth watching! An aerial competition is decided over two jumps, and points are awarded for the amount of "air" achieved (height and distance), for the difficulty and quality of the acrobatic manoeuvres, and for the safety of the landing. The jumps are performed off "kickers", which are built to varying heights and degrees of slope depending on the competitors' requirements. The run-in to the kicker provides the necessary speed: too much is as dangerous as too little, so competitors are allowed a number of dummy runs, up to the kicker but no further, to check snow conditions and ensure their speeds are correct. The landing area has a steep run-off, at a minimum of 37°.

Aerial enthusiasts begin by learning upright jumps (the "spread eagle", the "daffy", the "mule kick", the "backscratcher"), and work through twisting jumps (the "triple helicopter") before trying somersaults and finally combinations. At the highest level a winning jump will often include three twists and three somersaults before touching down. Obviously it takes a lot of practice under safe conditions to master such tricks, and so aerialists use trampolines to learn both specific techniques and general "air sense" – the feel for one's position in the air. During the off season they will also practise on water jumps, where the landing, though wetter than snow, is rather more soft.

BALLET In just over two minutes the ballet skier performs a self-selected routine to music, including not only difficult step movements (the "crossed waltz", for example), but also moves such as pirouettes, somersaults and handsprings, which use the poles for support. The event is much akin to figure skating, demanding a combination of athletic strength and balletic elegance, and competitors are judged not just on the technical difficulty of what they do, but also on aesthetics: their grace, smoothness and overall choreography.

SPEED SKIING

You would be forgiven for thinking the stars of the Flying Kilometre have come straight out of a space movie! But their achievement is very down to earth: speed skiers hold the record for the fastest unpowered means of travel by human beings, with speeds up to 139 mph, or 223 kph.

While their streamlined helmets and skintight suits may look like something out of a futuristic fiction, this quest for ultimate speed in fact goes back to the pioneering days of the sport. The first events were organized in Switzerland at St Moritz in the early 1930s. Between 1945 and 1975 the record breaking centred on Cervinia in Italy and Portillo in Chile, and more recently Les Arcs in France has been the place to be. It is at Les Arcs in fact that speed skiing will finally achieve the stamp of respectability in 1992. Traditionally the event has not enjoyed the popularity or success of the other ski disciplines. But the international skiing community has now recognized its legitimacy, with its inclusion as a demonstration sport in the next Winter Olympics.

<table>
<tr><td>SKI TIPS</td><td>Ride the tram-lines. The traverse is used to move diagonally across the slope. Skis are bent parallel and on the uphill edges to grip the snow. More weight is placed on the downhill ski. Try to leave tracks in the snow like a set of tram-lines.</td></tr>
</table>

While the outlandish wear of speed skiers has been specifically designed to reduce friction and drag to a minimum, certain other gimmicks in the search for speed have been outlawed. For example, some competitors fitted forward-view mirrors to their skis, so they could look down, make the shape of their tuck even more aerodynamic, and still see where they were going. Others have been known to have themselves bolted to sports car roofs, to practise technique at high speeds! This has also been outlawed in many countries, and those with enough money now hire wind tunnels instead.

This care for safety extends to the course itself, which has to be prepared with laborious precision. The surface must be consistent throughout, and the gradient, though extremely steep, made as smooth as possible. Competitors sidestep up the piste before an event, to avoid creating any last-minute undulations, and sometimes a water-filled balloon is even rolled down, to check that the camber of the slope will not make a skier veer off line. A sport in which the unshielded human body travels at such inhuman speeds has to be very conscious of its safety record.

MONOSKIING

When it comes to skiing, some people just can't be satisfied with the old-fashioned and traditional; especially, it seems, if they're American or French. The citizens of these two countries tend to lead the way in redefining the exotic and the experimental on snow.

Monoskis are a good example: an American invention taken up with relish in France. A champion surfer, Mike Doyle, collaborated with a Californian surfboard company to produce the prototype monoski; and whether you believe they are fad or innovation, there are a number of French manufacturers with hopes and fortunes riding on the success of the monoboard.

There are in fact certain advantages of one ski over two, because the skier's weight is spread over a much larger surface area. This achieves a floating effect in deep snow and in the slush of spring. Against this there are handling problems on ice, and having your skis "locked together" means that balance is reduced. The classic building blocks of good technique on two skis are just as important on one. But they have to be exaggerated: e.g. positive pole planting helps to improve the timing and balance of a monoski turn. When traversing the board tends to slip away, because the feet are locked square in a forward direction. So it is important to compensate with a more pronounced twist of the upper body down the slope.

Above all, though, the monoboard was invented to satisfy that little bit of escapism in each of us; and in powder they truly add a new dimension to the thrill.

SNOWBOARDING

Snowboarding is the craze which is sweeping out of the USA to resorts across the world, and it is now the biggest growth area in snow-related pastimes. Having been vilified by the traditionalists and worshipped by an exuberant collection of free spirits, the concept has taken flight on the ski slopes of Europe in the last year. As one of Britain's best snowboarders, Martyn Drayton, explained, "To be seen in Austria not so long ago with a snowboard would have been sacrilege. Now all Austrian ski

Snowboarding, or 'shredding', is where surfing meets skiing; it is the latest craze but is an enormous growth area and is here to stay.

instructors are required to have a working knowledge of the form, though they are not required to teach it."

With proper tuition he reckons you can be up and achieving the snowboard basics in two hours, and it bears little relation to any skiing ability. For unlike monoskiing, you ride a snowboard without poles, and with your feet strapped sideways; so the main influences on technique come from skateboarding and surfing. But Drayton emphasizes that with this "laid-back" image must go a determination to do things right in the mountains. Fun must go hand in hand with safety and respect for others around you. He knows that snowboarding has not had a good reputation, with the untutored picking up a board and proceeding to career round the slopes knocking people down. So his message is a simple one: have a go, but do it properly.

Inevitably it is in France that snowboarding has made its mark, though the sport was born out of an American idea. The first important work was carried out by Winterstick, a company from Salt Lake City. But the US ski authorities soon had other ideas about the new toy, with problems encountered when snowboarders hopped off lifts to "surf" in restricted areas. So in North American resorts the boards were promptly banned.

In France, however, snowboarding captured the imagination – and quickly found new twists to the original idea. Technically, the methods of attaching boots to the boards have improved immensely, while steel edges have been developed to improve contact on hard pisted snow. At the same time the competitive side of the sport has grown. Europe's traditional strength in the Alpine disciplines has created the new skill of slalom snowboarding, while in America the taste for surfing and skateboarding resulted in trick snowboarding as another strand to the sport.

But why stop there, some will say, when you can still find a few more variations on a theme? Ever heard of snow sailing? Yes: now you can mount a windsurf sail on a snowboard, for that little extra sense of speed!

ARTIFICIAL/DRY SLOPES

Something very British and very peculiar has happened in Britain, the rise of the dry ski slope. The first such, laid down 25 years ago, were very small, allowing hardly more than a couple of turns before you reached the end. But now some are as high as Nelson's Column, and plans are in the pipeline for multi-slope centres throughout the country. Already there are 66 slopes in England, 22 in Scotland, 10 in Wales and 4 in Northern Ireland. There are also artificial cross-country tracks, and even artificial mogul bumps have been incorporated at the South London centre, Profiles. It all makes substantial business sense, because as many of us will ski on a dry slope each winter as will go abroad.

But can skiing on a lattice-work of PVC bristle toothbrushes substitute for the real thing? Well, it is admittedly a far cry from deep powder. Nevertheless every technical element of skiing can be simulated on dry, and Britain is quickly finding that practice makes perfect. Of course an artificial slope cannot exactly recreate all the properties of snow. But it still gives people a chance to brush up throughout the year, before heading out with hard-earned cash for perhaps only a few days of the real thing.

An artificial slope provides an instant piste for both beginners and those who want to perfect their technique before heading for the snow.

Learning as a beginner on an artificial slope will also help make the most of those vital hours in the snow. For a start, the learner can get used to the strange sensation of deep-sea-diver-like boots, and of long planks of wood attached to his feet. Indeed all the movements of skiing can be developed on a dry slope, though the odd fall is probably rather more bruising on an artificial surface. But that will probably make you feel all the more at home on snow when you get there; and in fact after the greater friction of the dry slope many movements actually become easier on snow, which is inevitably more slippery. (All the same, various methods of lubricating dry slopes have been developed to improve their slickness. Many favour a water sprinkler system; so do not be surprised to see hardened ski fans out on the local slope after a rain storm – or in the middle of one!)

Experts and racers especially use waxes, to attain optimum efficiency and control. But for the more leisurely inclined fishscales are fine!

Dry slopes have been the subject of many sporting challenges, some serious, some not so. ITV's charity extravaganza Telethon saw the Gloucester and Chatham ski slopes battling it out for a 24 hour endurance record. The Kent slope eventually came out the winner, setting a world marathon record of more than 1,800 miles. There are now over 40 events on dry slopes in Britain each year.

But there are more authentic events, such as the annual British dry slope championships, which test the mettle of our finest youngsters. All of the current British development squad have come through their first experiences of skiing and their first races on plastic. With our climate, it's the only way.

Exercise can be taken at any level and at any age in cross-country skiing, where you are free to choose your own route and pace.

CROSS COUNTRY

While skiing has its roots in cross country (also known as Nordic, *ski de fond* or *langlauf*), nevertheless this style has been relatively neglected in recent times. Now, though, it is certainly on the way back. Perhaps people had been put off by the physical excesses of Nordic skiing as seen in the Winter Olympics, with the marathon in athletics seeming like a gentle stroll in comparison. But this has been to miss out on what the Scandinavian countries have enjoyed for many centuries. In northern Europe Nordic is recognized as a basic and efficient mode of transport, by which with a modicum of effort you can travel many miles over snow-covered terrain. In fact its roots hark back to a time when skiing in Scandinavia was a necessity of life. There are records which suggest that the Vikings used a rudimentary ski, and much later it was Norwegian emigrants who spread the use of cross-country skis to the new worlds of Australia and North America.

One basic criterion makes cross country different from Alpine skiing: the latter only deals with skiing in downhill mode, where Nordic involves a range of abilities and skills, which allow the skier to propel himself along the flat, uphill and down again. But another difference flows from this: the far greater freedom of cross country, without dependence on ski lifts and tows. This is an element which recreational skiers are finding has appeal to all standards and all ages. Quite simply, Nordic skiing can be a country stroll, if you want it to be. Pack a picnic, make a day of it, and most important have the time to take in some of the most breathtaking scenery in the world. In a growing trend, many Alpine resorts are now making provision for cross-country tracks. These are double-grooved paths in which the cross-country skis slot. Usually there are two sets (like a dual carriageway), for skiers going in opposite directions. The trails cater for all levels of exertion, they can be as easy or as testing as you want to make them – and one of the enduring pleasures is the absence of lift queues!

Beyond the prepared ski routes there are two other facets to cross country: ski touring and racing. Both are very common in Scandinavia. Touring involves skiers breaking their own trail, and routes can vary from an afternoon's outing to trips lasting many days. On the most popular touring trails there are numerous mountain huts and shelters for overnight stops. Another common sight is the *pulk*, a simple sledge and harness device, for extra provisions, which a skier can pull.

Racing is another Scandinavian obsession and not just the preserve of an athletic élite. There are Citizen races, in which a field of more than ten thousand may set out over distances of up to 90 kilometres. The route can take more than eight hours to complete and, like the marathon-running craze, draws not only people who want to win but also those who just want to say they have done it! The Swedish Vasaloppet is the oldest cross-country marathon. Founded in 1922, the 89 kilometre (55 mile) race attracts a huge entry for a journey between Sälen and Mora in central Sweden on the first Sunday in March. This race makes up just one tenth of the celebrated World Loppet series. The other nine are the Dolomitenlauf, Marcialonga, König Ludwig Lauf, Gatineau 55, Transjurassienne, American Birkebeiner, Finlandia Hiihto, Engadin Skimarathon, Birkebeinerrennet and Sapporo International Ski Marathon in Japan.

SKI TIPS	Bumps. The skier absorbs the bump by flexing the legs and at the same time obtains support from a strong pole plant, creating a compression turn. The skis are pivoted in a new direction as the legs are extended to maintain snow control.

There are many ways to throw yourself off a mountain – and not all of them involve skis. As seen here parapenting is one of the more exhilarating.

Top-class races take place over anything between 15 and 90 kilometres, including both men's and women's events and both individual and relay. There are also the multi-skill events peculiar to Nordic sport, the biathlon and the combined. The biathlon has its roots in times past when settlers had to be both swift on skis and accurate with a rifle in order to hunt, eat, and survive. The World Cup distance is 20 kilometres, made up of five laps of a prepared circuit. Four times during the race the competitors must stop at a specified shooting range to fire five shots. Missed targets add a penalty to their overall time. Sports physiologists believe that biathlon skiers are some of the fittest athletes of any sport. One product of superb fitness is the ability to reduce one's heartbeat quickly after strenuous activity – so achieving the calm and collected state which is a basic requirement for shooting a rifle accurately. Finally the Nordic combined is part ski jumping and part cross country and only open to men.

CROSS-COUNTRY SKIS

With the exception of cross-country ski poles (which have to be long enough to provide the push to a forward stride on the flat) cross-country equipment is much lighter than its Alpine equivalent, and generally cheaper. Skis vary in type, depending on the kind of cross-country skiing involved. Wood was the traditional material, but it has now been superseded by fibreglass and plastic. A general-purpose ski is about 50 mm wide, while training and racing skis are lighter and narrower. Metal-edged skis, slightly narrower than Alpine ones, are used for mountain touring where the skier needs more purchase and "cut" into the snow on a steep slope, and for telemarking – a slalom race using the elegant telemark turn which is performed by cross-country skiers on a steep descent.

There is also a choice between waxable and waxless skis. The innovation which really produced a resurgence in cross-country skiing among the general public was the introduction of the waxless or "fishscale" ski. The latter name refers to the pattern embossed in the middle section of the ski sole. Other ideas to the same purpose include mohair strips fixed into the sole with the nap facing backwards. These grip the snow as the skier pushes off, but cause little resistance when the ski is gliding. Mica chips set in the sole work on the same principle. Both these other versions have now largely given way to the fishscale; but in all cases there is a ridge effect, cutting into the snow, so that the ski cannot slip backwards.

Though fishscales and the like cause some unwanted friction, the traditional alternative is far more troublesome. Before these developments, grip waxing was the only way to stop the skis sliding backwards when taking a forward step. Different waxes would be applied depending on the type of snow conditions and temperature. Today the procedure still holds at competition level, and generally among cross-country skiers of higher ability. Some of the tools of the trade include gas burner, cork, spatulas, wax removers and scrapers, as well as a wide and confusing range of different waxes for different purposes, temperatures and conditions. Applying a wax properly, and picking the right wax or combination of waxes for the job, is something that only comes with long practice. In the meantime for the less diligent it can be a tedious procedure, and one liable to error.

Waxable skis are not now used by beginners. But the majority of cross-country specialists would say that if you want to ski well, you have to use waxable skis eventually. Even as a beginner, you may find yourself wanting to have a go when only waxable skis are on offer; so here are a few hints about preparing them. The front and rear ends of a ski's sole, the two areas most in contact with the snow, are waxed so as to achieve the best possible gliding performance. The glide wax to be used depends on temperature conditions, and there is an international colour coding to guide your choice. Meanwhile the central section, which only touches the snow when weighted, needs an application of grip wax. This will allow snow crystals to penetrate the wax layer, thereby supplying friction.

Again, depending on conditions, different waxes are needed to help this process along. Grip waxes come in two types. There are hard waxes, which come in stick form, and are used on fresh (unchanged) snow; and there are soft "klister" waxes, which come in tubes, and are used on changed snow – snow which has melted, and perhaps refrozen. As with glide waxes, both types of grip wax conform to an international colour code. With stick waxes, a green category wax is used with temperatures up to –10°C, blue up to –2°C, violet to zero and red above zero. With klister waxes, green and blue are used for snow that has melted and refrozen, violet and red for snow that has melted and not refrozen.

Skis also benefit from preparation, however, before waxes are applied. There are still a few wooden skis around, and for these an application of tar protects the base from moisture. (Also, no glide wax is used on wooden skis, grip wax is applied over the entire length.) But almost all recreational skiers who now take up cross country will be using synthetic skis, which have an epoxy-resin coating, and these will benefit from a preliminary treatment with glide wax. It is applied as a hot wax and then scraped off, leaving a fine layer which smoothes out any rough textures.

After pre-treatment, wax at room temperature if possible, making sure the skis are dry and clean. Try the colder waxes first if you are unsure of the prevailing conditions. Waxes of the warmer codings will subsequently adhere to a cold wax base, but this is not the case the other way round. Several thin layers are better than one thick one.

Boots and Bindings

If you decide to take up cross country, then you may want to buy boots fairly early on. After all, it's the same as with a pair of walking boots or running shoes: after a few kilometres a good fit becomes fairly important! In general the boots for cross country are sturdy but supple and soft. They are far less cumbersome than the Alpine hard plastic boot and, attached only at the toe, clip into a simple binding. A word of caution, though: not all bindings fit all boots. This is why you have to be careful about buying or hiring cross-country skis and boots separately. For a start, different types of boot and associated binding have been developed for different purposes. Low-cut boots like running shoes are best for prepared tracks and competition skiing. But if you are going off-trail, as in ski touring, higher, sturdier, more robust boots are needed to give better protection against the snow. Even within these basic types, though, different manufacturers have come up with different binding arrangements. At one time there was at least some standardization on a 75mm Nordic norm for off-trail bindings, but in the last two or three seasons even this has largely gone by the board. Most manufacturers now have their own boot-binding systems for different purposes; so you need to get advice and choose carefully.

Clothing

Clothing for cross country partly depends on which form of the activity you find yourself undertaking. The typical *langlauf* track is usually located in the shelter of the mountain valley floor, and in these conditions cross-country skiing with its steady exertion can be hot work. The same principles apply as for any day out in the mountains: thin layers are the key, with perhaps a windcheater over the top. For trousers, tracksuit bottoms will do, or lightweight salopettes or ski pants. The alternative is the specialized all-in-one skintight suit – which is likely to look aerodynamic but feel hot. Of course, adequate hat and gloves are just as important in Nordic as they are in Alpine skiing.

For ski touring, however, you will need to prepare with more care: carry clothes adequate for any conditions, expected or unexpected. Get expert advice, for once you head off into untracked snow you are dealing with a hostile environment. It only needs a sudden change in the weather to make matters very serious for the unprepared.

Cross-Country Basics

Most of those new to cross country begin on a simple prepared trail. They're often found near towns and cities in Scandinavia, but also these days at many Alpine resorts. A simple ski ramble on such a prepared track is not dangerous and is not difficult. In effect it is a walk on snow. Often there is a parallel double track to keep your skis on the right path, so even steering is no problem. With the cross-country binding holding the toe but leaving the heel free to move, the basic movement is the same as walking, and with practice this becomes a glide with opposing arm and leg working in combination. Most prepared trails have been designed to flatten out the more fatiguing and technically more difficult climbs, but simple gradients, with waxless skis especially, can be taken quite literally in your stride. The reverse camber of the fishscale pattern will dig in and stop the skis sliding backwards. Only, to maintain balance uphill, you will find yourself shortening your stride pattern and using the poles for greater support.

SKI TIPS	Snowplough. Skis are placed in a V-shape, slightly on their inside edges. Keep them equally weighted. Speed is dictated by the width of the V.

As your skill develops you will begin to tackle steeper gradients, either by side stepping or using the herringbone technique. This is rather like a reverse snowplough, as you face up the fall line with ski tips splayed out and tails together. In fact of course the principle is the same, since the wedge you've created stops you from slipping back. For greater speed over flat terrain the double pole push is the basic technique: feet together and both poles planted and pushed through simultaneously. As for turning on a downslope, cross-country skiers accomplish this in a variety of ways. Many of the manoeuvres are in fact the same as Alpine techniques: the snowplough, the stem christie (which of course originated in cross-country skiing), the step turn, and sometimes parallel turns. The main difference is in equipment. Soft, supple shoes do not give as much support to the lower leg as ski boots, the skis are narrow and edgeless (unless you have a metal-edged touring/telemark ski), and the bindings do not fix your heels. With less control, therefore, make turns more slowly, and do not expect such extravagant Alpine results.

The form of turn that is particular to cross country, though, is the telemark, and this once-neglected technique has experienced a tremendous revival in interest in recent years. In fact this nineteenth-century Norwegian innovation has become, a hundred years later, a cult craze in the USA.

THE TELEMARK AND TELEMARKING

This method of turning was developed in the 1860s by Sondre Norheim, of the Telemark region of Norway – hence the name. The skier initiates the turn by bending his knees and allowing his inside (uphill) ski to trail the outside (downhill). The manoeuvre is very stable, since the skier is lowering his centre of gravity, and with toe-only bindings this gives far better balance on a descent. It becomes especially useful when the skier has a heavy rucksack on his back, and in fact this is how the telemark resurgence began in the 1970s, when mountain touring took off in America. Of course the technique was originally developed for wooden skis, but it has particularly benefitted from the changes in ski technology, since metal-edged skis cut into the slopes to give far better control.

The revived interest has in turn produced a new cult sport, telemarking. This is a downhill slalom race in which only telemark turns are allowed. Again, of course, metal-edged synthetic skis are used. The whole thing is inevitably frowned on by purists! But they agree in seeing the telemark as the classic form of cross-country downhill turn.

Ski Touring

Ski touring is perhaps the classic form of skiing as it was practised before the invention of lifts! It is a synthesis of all the skiing skills, both cross country and downhill, plus physical and mental fitness and a bit of climbing technique. Crucially touring requires skill, stamina and mountain craft, while the rewards are the discovery of an untouched beauty. Trekking in a group from hut to mountain hut means that companionship and teamwork are of the essence. Fitness is important too. If you are unused to the day-long physical demands of touring at high altitudes, do make sure you prepare well and give yourself time to acclimatize. Competence may be required in any skiing conditions from perfect powder to breakable crust. Ski touring is very much a matter of destinations reached rather than skiing style on the way, and there is a heavy premium placed on skiing efficiently and safely. Falls are tiring and could endanger the rest of the group.

Clothing requirements for ski touring are based on the sound principle of layering for warmth, with the outer layers providing proper windproofing and water resistance as necessary. A good sun cream with a strong filter factor, and good sunglasses, are also essential. As for skis, these are lighter than the Alpine variety. But other than that there are many similarities, especially with the "softer" Alpine skis designed for deep powder, which are flexible in the tip. Boots are rather like fell-walking boots. In the course of an "expedition" they need to provide suppleness for the gliding motions of cross-country and the telemark turn, support and strength for downhill skiing, and comfort for hiking. (If you go one stage further, into what is called "ski mountaineering", then even more adaptable footwear is needed, for if necessary the boots must be able to take crampons for climbing.)

Mountain resorts provide the perfect spot for relaxing while eating and sunbathing.

Proper bindings are also fundamental to mountain touring. They need to function as a competent safety binding for the downhill sections, enabling the ski to release during a bad fall. But the binding must also be able to act like its cross-country equivalent, attaching only the toe while allowing the heel to move freely. Most important, it must be able to function in extremes of cold, unaffected by a build-up of snow in the mechanism or under the boot sole. The importance of ski waxes has been dealt with already, but another modification which enables very steep uphill gradients to be negotiated are "skins" applied to the ski soles. Originally seal skin was used, but now artificial fabric clip-on or stick-on alternatives are available which give the ski sole plenty of grip.

Basic climbing tools are essential in case of emergencies: rope, harness, ice axe, etc. Equally important is such safety equipment as avalanche bleepers, first-aid supplies and emergency rations. Survival in unguarded, isolated mountain terrain requires avalanche awareness (see the avalanche section in the chapter on Safety), but it also demands the sound judgement of a competent guide or experienced mountaineers in the party.

CHAPTER FIVE

Safety

Care on the Slopes: an Introduction to Safety

The risk of accident on the slopes is being reduced all the time. Modern boots and bindings limit the chances of a broken leg, while resorts pay constant attention to the quality of their ski runs and the dangers of avalanche. Over a decade or so the chances of injury have fallen by 40 per cent, say the insurers. Now it's believed the incidence of injury is only about one per 250 skiing days. To minimize your own chances of accident here are a few common-sense rules to stick to:

Children are taught to regard safety as paramount in their ski classes.

* Never ski alone.

* Make sure that equipment, whether your own or hired, has been correctly adjusted to your weight, height and skiing standard. It is particularly worth checking every day that the bindings are releasing properly. Grit, dirt and constant use can sometimes effect the mechanism.
* Note the weather before each day's skiing. Take adequate clothing because conditions can change. Take a hat, even if you keep it stuffed in a pocket – till you need it. The head if unprotected is the body's greatest source of heat loss.
* Sun and heat can affect you as well as cold. Carry a strong sun cream and lip salve.
* At all times take notice of the piste signs.
* When skiing off-piste ensure that all of your party are wearing avalanche rescue devices.
* Get proper exercise *before* you go on holiday. The fitter you are the less likely you are to have a fall.
* And, just in case: make sure your insurance policy gives you sufficient cover and includes an adequate third-party/personal-liability clause.
* To reiterate the advice of the Ski Club of Great Britain, heed these precautions along with the FIS code printed below, for your own sake and that of other skiers. It is important to ski with respect for the mountains and those who live there, and to do so will help maintain the good reputation of British skiers abroad.

THE FIS CODE OF CONDUCT

This ten-point code has been in existence since the late 1960s and was conceived by the International Ski Federation as a guide to common sense on the slopes. With skiing becoming ever more popular, its provisions have never been more apposite. They are not law, but rather guidelines to good behaviour. Nevertheless lack of respect for the code has been used to back up court cases concerning accidents on the slopes.

The FIS Code states: Skiing is a sport and as such it contains both elements of risk and penal responsibilities.

1 RESPECT FOR OTHERS. A skier shall conduct himself in such a way that he does not endanger or prejudice others.

2 SPEED AND WAY OF SKIING. A skier must adapt his speed and his way of skiing to his personal ability as well as to the prevailing conditions of ground and weather.

3 CHOICE OF COURSE. A skier coming from above must choose his course in such a way that he assures the safety of the skier below.

4 OVERTAKING. It is permitted to overtake another skier going down or up, to the right or left, but a wide margin must be given to the skier being overtaken to permit him to make his turns.

5 OBLIGATIONS FOR SKIERS FURTHER DOWN AND SKIERS CROSSING THE PISTE. A skier wishing to enter a downhill piste or cross such a piste must, by looking up and down, assure himself that he can do so without danger to himself or others. The same goes for a skier starting again after a stop on the piste.

6 STOPPING ON THE PISTE. A skier must avoid, if not absolutely necessary, stopping on the course especially at narrow passages or at places with bad visibility. After a fall, the skier must as soon as possible leave the course free.

7 CLIMBING. A climbing skier may use only one side of the piste. In bad visibility he cannot even do this. The same goes for a skier who is descending on foot.

8 RESPECT FOR THE SIGNS. Every skier must respect the signs on a downhill piste.

9 CONDUCT AT ACCIDENTS. At accidents everybody is duty-bound to assist.

10 IDENTIFICATION. Everybody who is a witness, responsible or not, to an accident, is required to establish his identity.

Resort Markings and Lift Systems

Skiers should be thoroughly aware of the piste signs, not only because they are one of the matters highlighted in the FIS code of conduct, but also because they have been placed there to further your skiing enjoyment and keep you safe from unseen hazards.

Piste maps are an essential part of a skier's everyday kit. As they say – never leave home without one. Normally they are given out when you buy a lift pass, but they are also generally available at the major lifts in the resort. Some resorts publish them in different languages. The maps show the whole ski area, marking ski runs, restaurants, ski lifts and routes back to the village. Pistes will be shown according to a colour-coded system common to most of Europe. Green is very easy, blue is beginner to intermediate, red is more difficult and black is very difficult. Some resorts bracket green with blue runs. When looking for a route across a resort make sure the runs do not change colour (and therefore standard) beyond your own accomplishments.

Piste signs do vary between resorts, and without them it is easy to become disorientated or lost. On the first couple of days become accustomed not only to the mountain but also to the type of signs to expect. In the large ski areas, which might encompass ten resorts (e.g. Portes du Soleil and Les Trois Vallées), there are strategic signposts detailing the routes towards linking villages. Elsewhere there are usually signs back to the resort centre. Marker poles show the position of prepared pistes. These are essential in poor visibility, and it is important to learn the resort's system of deployment. Some place them in the centre of the piste, others locate them down each side. In the latter method there is often some distinguishing mark to show whether you are on the left- or right-hand side of the piste. Marker poles are usually the colour of the piste grade (green, blue, red or black) and may be marked with a number which descends in value as you head downhill. In the case of an accident, or if you have dropped something from a chairlift, look out for a pole number to locate the site accurately.

All ski lifts are marked on the piste map; keep one handy at all times to avoid getting lost.

Deep snow requires an adaptation of normal skiing techniques. The skier tends to keep the skis evenly weighted and adjusts the stance backwards and forwards to allow them to rise to the surface for the next turn.

SKI TIPS

Yellow and black poles crossed in the snow indicate an obstruction, e.g. rocks or ice. These colours are also used to rope off areas. Such barriers have been put there for a purpose, and it is a constant source of exasperation to the ski patrols when their warnings are ignored. After all, they are only there to keep us out of trouble. The key word is patience. The piste has probably been closed with the danger of avalanches in mind. Often after heavy snowfalls lifts remain closed even in fine weather for the same reason. In some resorts the ski patrols have the authority to cancel a ski pass for an hour or half a day – or even permanently – if they have seen a skier flagrantly ignoring official signs.

Insurance

While modern boots and bindings make leg injuries less likely, sadly the statistics show that four per cent of us will still get into a scrape. Problems are most usually caused by carelessness, often due to fatigue, and increasingly involve collisions between skiers, so nobody should ski without adequate insurance. If you are injured medical expenses are high, while if you have caused an accident you could be sued for considerable sums. That has been the way of it for many years in the USA, and unfortunately it is becoming increasingly common in Europe too.

Here is an example of a policy with only minimum cover.

MEDICAL EXPENSES: £50,000. To include rescue from the slopes by stretcher, snow cat or, most expensive of all, helicopter. Recent estimates of the cost of a helicopter rescue flight put it at £15 a minute. There are also visits to the doctor, hospital bills, and possibly repatriation by air ambulance to cover against. The policy should also give an emergency telephone number back in the British Isles.

PERSONAL ACCIDENT: £10,000. For provision against death, loss of a limb, and permanent total disability. You should also consider indemnity against loss of earnings.

PERSONAL LIABILITY: £500,000. This is most important and should cover you against skiing into others or causing property damage. These may seem big figures, but in fact this is minimum recommended cover and the premiums are quite cheap.

AVALANCHES

If you want to enjoy the last run home, you must understand that the mountains are a harsh and extreme environment. From the most innocuous beginnings an avalanche can become a fearsome and irresistible force rolling down thousands of tons of snow, ice and debris. One cubic metre of snow weighs one metric tonne. All the people who live and work in the mountains will tell you that they know how easily disaster can strike and that they will do everything in their power to come to a skier's rescue. In the Alps the *pisteurs* are the men on the front line, and backing them up comes a huge support system of communications and transport. This will include helicopters, which do not come cheap. The cost of a rescue falls on the rescued, and it is worth making certain that your insurance will cover all eventualities.

Attention to avalanche safety is the same the world over. In the fabled North American snow of Colorado and Utah there is an average of 450 inches during the season. At the resort of Snowbird, where avalanche is a constant threat, the ski patrolmen are quick to blow away the danger with self-propelled artillery shells. Like others in America they work under the constant threat of litigation. Over there a person's proven blame will very quickly result in them being sued for amounts running into telephone numbers; and if the resort management could be to blame the American solution is to sue them too. So when Snowbird or any other American resort has any doubts about snow pack weakness, on or off the piste, it will not risk opening those parts of the mountains – even if it means keeping them closed the whole season.

Throughout a resort pisteurs are located at main lift junctions to provide help and first aid if needed. Here, at the Austrian resort of Solden, their hut can be seen beside the lift building.

In Europe the prevailing attitude leaves it up to individuals to get on with their lives and their sport, in the fervent hope that they and fellow skiers will not be endangered. If you talk to the professionals, however, like the Zimmer brothers who run a specialist school in off-piste tours and tuition (Top Ski at Val d'Isère), they will recount their frustration at the lack of discipline and knowledge of many who take off into the more isolated areas. There are, and will be, fatalities every year off the beaten track. A Europe not yet ruled by lawyers will, for the time being, uphold skiers' right to risk their own lives in order to challenge the deep powder. No one in the Alpine ski business wants to see the American model replicated in the Alps, as long as ignorance can be replaced with common sense.

Without being alarmist about the risks, there is plenty of simple and practical advice available from people who know what they're talking about. For me some time spent with Fred Harper, adviser to the Ski Club of Great Britain and one of only a handful of non-French mountain guides at that capital of *Alpinisme*, Chamonix, was very much of an eye opener. First he pointed out that avalanches happen primarily on slopes of between 25° and 45°; the angle of slope is fundamental to whether or not an avalanche could occur. Off-piste slopes below 25° are challenge enough for many powder skiers, and here there is little likelihood of avalanche. The shape of a slope also has a large bearing: a concave slope has an inherent structural stability which a convex one does not. After a heavy, wind-blown snowfall off-piste areas should as a general rule be left well alone for more than a day to allow the snow pack to settle and stabilize. North- and east-facing Alpine slopes are in the lee of prevailing wind patterns; so this is where the best powder settles but also where there is most danger of a "wind slab" building up. Rapid changes in temperature also induce instability. A continuing problem can arise if there is a warm start to the season, which prevents a permanent cold base becoming established. At any time rapid thaws are dangerous: watch out for the effect of afternoon sun on south and west slopes.

When skiing keep away from gullies and from routes which lead below large overhangs of snow (cornices). Check for anchorage, e.g. thick trees and protruding rocks, which will have a bearing on how a slide could develop. In the Swiss resort of Saas Fee the ski holiday business has brought its own problems. The community has neglected its farming traditions for more lucrative tourist services, with the result that fewer sheep and cattle have been grazed on the high summer pastures. With Nature's own prodigious lawnmowers having less impact on the mountain grass, an unforeseen problem has built up in the winter, since uncut grass provides less anchorage for the snow cover. Hence in the last couple of years there has been an abrupt resurgence in Saas Fee's pastoral enthusiasms.

Before attempting an off-piste trip check the avalanche forecasts. Go in a group (mountain guides recommend at least six to a party), and make sure you are all equipped with transceivers. (They can be hired from the Ski Club of Great Britain.) Each transceiver must be kept set to transmit ("send"). Then, in the event of avalanche burial, the survivors set theirs to receive, and quarter the area for signals, starting at the last point at which a skier was seen and then working down the line of slide. The closer the receiver gets to the buried skier the louder the noise. Recco radar reflectors are now also quite common, stitched into ski clothes and boots. But these do not send a signal, they are passive. Detection depends on the resort having access to a Recco detector, and so far few do.

Skiing off-piste means you can enjoy fresh powder snow – but make sure you do not go alone.

Skidding. This is the first manoeuvre in which the skier learns to turn with parallel skis. From a steeper traverse the skis are flattened and turned across the direction of travel to create a skid.

SKI TIPS

If there is a slide a lot depends on the shape of the slope. Any gullies or holes will quickly fill up, burying anyone unfortunate enough to have been swept in under tons of debris. On the other hand a long even slope causes an avalanche to fan out, with less depth. Statistically, a skier buried more than two metres deep has relatively little chance of survival. In the event of being caught in a slide, experts suggest that your chances of survival are improved if you try to ski at 45° to the fall line. Get behind a tree trunk or rock if you can. If you are swept away, jettison your skis and attempt to roll away from the avalanche.

Illness, Injury and Accident

COLD The effects of the cold are nothing new – the earliest evidence of frostbite dates back 5,000 years to a pre-Columbian mummy found in the Chilean mountains! There are always several factors at work: the temperature, the wind speed and the precipitation if any (in the mountains that is likely to be snow, but the possibility of rain should not be ruled out). Wind chill is a specific element which skiers should understand. The cooling effect of a given air temperature on the human body is greatly increased in the presence of wind, and likewise the speed a skier moves produces exactly the same result. With a wind speed of 20 mph (32 kph) and an air temperature of –14°C, the wind chill equivalent could be as much as –34°C.

FROSTNIP is a superficial injury causing numbness along with a pallor or whitening of exposed skin. The most vulnerable areas are those which are furthest from the heart's blood supply: the face, especially the nose and ears, are difficult to protect, while the fingers are another cold spot. This is a very prevalent problem among skiers because these points are likely to be exposed to cold fast-moving air. Simple warming can be effected by the pressure of a warm hand or by putting the hands under the armpits.

FROSTBITE This is a deeper injury with destruction of the affected tissue to varying levels. It is usually encountered at temperatures below freezing, but be warned that it can also occur above freezing due to the factors already mentioned: snow fall, wind velocity and duration of exposure.

HYPOTHERMIA This is a condition where the body cannot generate heat as fast as it is losing it. Unlike frostbite the effect is not localized, indeed it is the general body core temperature which is reduced below normal (37.5°C). Though not a common condition, skiers can nevertheless become affected after long exposure to inclement conditions. Other factors which have a bearing are exhaustion, inadequate clothing, the quality of shelter if for any reason you cannot continue skiing, and your intake of food. The aptly named "buddy system" is important, with each of the party looking for any signs of deterioration in their partners. It is quite possible that if one person becomes affected, the others are not far behind. In extreme cases the signs and symptoms include irrational behaviour, with sudden intermittent bursts of energy and then lethargy. Responses are likely to become slow, and there may be fits of uncontrolled shivering, loss of co-ordination, headaches and blurred vision.

To treat the problem, find shelter from the wind, insulate the patient from the ground, and apply warmth by huddling together. But it is important that warmth is also derived from the inside if possible; warming someone in a hypothermic condition only from the outside simply drives cold blood into the body core. Warm fluids are therefore important, along with sugary foods. But do not use alcohol, which opens up the blood vessels near the skin surface thereby increasing the rate of heat loss. When applying warmth externally, concentrate on those areas where the blood is closest to the skin surface: the pit of the stomach, the small of the back, the armpits, the back of the neck, the wrists and between the thighs. A foil ("space") blanket is valuable, and it is always well worth carrying one with you. They take up little space when folded and can fit easily into a pocket. Anyone who has seen the end of a marathon will know what they look like.

SNOW BLINDNESS Eyes are sensitive to the glare from snow and ice, and it does not necessarily need to be a sunny day for them to be affected, since snow reflects 80 per cent of ultra-violet light. Snow blindness will cause eyes to blink and squint, and to feel as though there is sand in them. Vision takes on a pink or reddish hue. If these effects occur, rest your eyes in a dark place and soothe the irritation with a cool wet cloth. But much more sensibly, eliminate the possibility of eye irritation by wearing a good-quality pair of sunglasses or goggles. Which is worse, damage to your eyes or a giant panda look to your sun tan?

EFFECTS OF ALTITUDE The body needs to acclimatize to height because oxygen in the atmosphere decreases with altitude. In lower-lying resorts this should not be a problem of course. Medically it is accepted that the effects of altitude begin at about 8,000 feet (approximately 2,400 metres). The signs of altitude sickness can include headaches, nausea, lethargy, dizziness and muscle weakness. These are the more extreme symptoms, but it is quite common to find sleeping difficult and to be affected by breathlessness during the day. The effects are exacerbated by rapid ascent (e.g. in a ski lift), so when you are going skiing at high levels remember not to rush, take your time.

EMERGENCY SHELTER

Be wary of the general effects of extreme cold: it is easy to withdraw from reality and thinking can become sluggish. The cold dulls the mind so keep active and bright. If in an extreme case you have been left on the mountain, or the weather has taken a real turn for the worse, then the only solution is shelter. But if a mountain hut or the lift operator's hut is not at hand, there are a couple of emergency solutions. You can consider the spaces left beneath the spreading boughs of the conifer trees (remember to get onto the lee side); otherwise, if there is a firm drift of snow nearby and protection is urgent, you can "snow hole". Dig into the side of the drift, and if possible make two levels. You shelter or sleep on the higher level since hot air rises, while the lower level traps the cold air which sinks. Remember too to make a hole through the roof for ventilation. If you may have to stay there for some time, use a block of snow as a door. But make sure it is loose fitting and position it inside the snow hole so that it cannot freeze and jam.

All these tips are only immediate thoughts to consider. Any cold injury also needs medical advice. Along with the cold there is also the potential risk of an accident.

ACCIDENTS In the event of an accident it is vital to keep calm. If a person has been immobilized by a collision or fall, mark the area by placing crossed skis a few metres above the site. This is not only a warning to others to keep clear. It will also gain the attention of any competent first-aiders, ski instructors, or ski patrols on the hill.

If there is a significant injury make the person comfortable, removing the skis only if it is possible to do so without moving injured limbs. Keep the patient warm (some ideas have already been explored in relation to cold injuries) and send at least one competent skier down the mountain to get help. Make sure the messenger goes with accurate details of where the accident has occurred; e.g. look for a piste marker number. Evacuation will be either by sled, otherwise happily known as the blood wagon, or in extreme conditions by helicopter (so make sure your insurance will cover the cost of one as they are not cheap).

In the event of serious injury, the priorities are the first aid ABC: airways, breathing, circulation. First make sure the airways are clear: look in the mouth and throat for foreign bodies preventing the passage of air, such as false teeth or snow. Then check that the victim is breathing. If not, apply artificial respiration, mouth to mouth. Check for the pulse at wrist or neck. If there is none, administer cardiac massage.

If the victim is bleeding apply firm pressure to the injured area. If the injured person is conscious try to establish the extent of injury and pain, to relay to the rescue services. Any movement of a back or spine injury could make matters worse. Assuming that they are not suffering from extreme cold, do not give anyone who may have a fracture or who might require surgery any food or drink, not even alcohol or sugared tea. Anyone who is unconscious should be turned on their side into the recovery position with the head tilted backwards to prevent the tongue or vomit blocking the airway.

Fitness

Skiing is one of the most demanding forms of exercise. Yet most of us will have to admit that, after a year minus one week's inactivity, we arrive back on the slopes pretty well unprepared for a rigorous seven days of using muscles which at any other time are barely flexed! Quite simply, there is a general sporting maxim which applies: "don't ski to get fit; get fit to ski!".

But getting fit does not have to be an arduous slog of sweat and pain. After all, that's not what we're going to be going on a skiing holiday for; so it doesn't make much sense to make ourselves miserable beforehand. It does, however, make sense to give ourselves an improved chance of enjoying our skiing, of being safer, and of being more resilient. There is nothing worse than being too weary to ski and to find that our ability is deteriorating through fatigue – quite apart from becoming more prone to injury. The only uncomfortable fact about learning to ski is that the process is likely to expend more energy than when technique and style have been established. At first too much effort is used making ineffective movements. So general all-round fitness is very necessary from the outset, while specific conditioning becomes more of a priority only as skiing skill improves.

Ideally you should maintain an acceptable level of fitness throughout the year, and any exercise is better than none. But with perhaps a couple of months to go and the ski slopes in mind, it is then certainly time to attend to specific ski fitness. As with any active sport, this involves four separate components.

ENDURANCE, or stamina, is the ability to repeat the same movement consistently over a period of time. Stamina can be built up by brisk walking, jogging, running, cycling, swimming or rope skipping; think about spending a minimum of 20 minutes twice a week doing one or more of the above. A home exerciser such as a rowing machine, exercise cycle or jogger (rebounder) is another idea. If time is limited, try to incorporate some extra effort into everyday activities. Leave the car in the parking space and walk perhaps? Climb the stairs instead of taking the lift? Working the heart and lungs for cardiovascular fitness will reduce breathlessness from long periods of exertion, speed up your recuperation from constant activity and help deal with the effects of thin air at altitude.

Other exercises aim to increase strength, flexibility and speed, and some suggestions for these follow.

STRENGTH is the maximum force which muscles can exert while repeating a movement. Strength is beneficial in performing athletic turns and in holding good skiing posture. Strong muscles also give better support to bones and joints.

FLEXIBILITY of joints promotes increased range of movement and control. Good flexibility is a safety measure which will reduce the chance of muscle tears and pulls. In fact flexibility exercises are not only important before a ski holiday, but should also be an integral part of a morning's preparations (along with clearing a hangover) before skiing. Stretching and warming down at the end of the day also help alleviate the build up of stiffness.

SPEED is the body's ability to move swiftly and to react to sudden changes in circumstances. It is difficult to exercise for specifically, but generally develops as a by-product of strength and flexibility within the context of your growing competence at a sport.

Exercises should at all times be interesting, so work on alternatives, don't be too rigid, and find out what the local sports centre can offer. Whether you decide to train at home or in a group, it is worth attending a class at first to be certain of exercising properly. Poor technique is potentially dangerous. Above all, if you are in any doubt about an exercise programme or have a medical condition, consult your doctor first.

Here are a few offerings. Pick the ones which suit you and, to increase the benefit of a programme, gradually work on the intensity and effort you put into the exercises, and their duration and frequency. The experts say initial exercise should be gentle but positive, so that success in the early stages is both physically and mentally stimulating.

WARM-UP EXERCISES
A proper warm-up reduces the chance of injury and stimulates the heart and lungs to be ready for activity.

JOG in gentle repetitions of about 30 seconds at a time, walking for 30 seconds in between. Also jog on the spot, lifting knees to touch your fingers. Alternatively use a "home jogger" (rebounder), so avoiding the danger of impact injury.

STRETCHES should work through the body bit by bit: rolling the head; circling arms, shoulders and hips; stretching the legs by hugging each knee in turn and then by grasping each foot and gently pulling backwards. Finally an all-round stretch begins with the arms straight above the head. Follow a sweeping pendulum movement down, and finish in a tuck position with the stomach just touching the thighs (not a full squat which is bad for the knees).

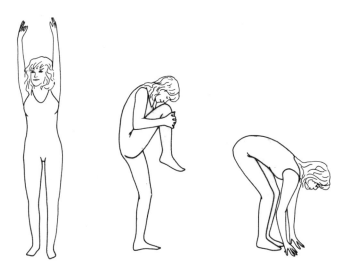

STRONGER STUFF

Do remember to start gently and proceed gradually! You're aiming at fitness, not at pulled muscles or a strained back. You want to enjoy your holiday, not spend it in hospital.

PRESS UPS. Start with hands shoulder-width apart, and lower the body with a straight back. Go as low as you can without the body touching the floor, then return to the start position. As a change from normal press ups, place the hands splayed outwards. Remember to build up slowly, increasing the number of repetitions over a period of weeks. This exercise will strengthen the shoulder girdle and the triceps, which when skiing can ache with unaccustomed use from poling over any flat bits.

SIT UPS, or trunk curls. Lie on your back with your legs close together, knees flexed and off the floor. Straighten arms on top of thighs and sit up to touch your knees with your hands. To increase the difficulty fold your arms across your chest and later clasp your hands behind your neck, and as you sit up bring your knees up and touch them with your elbows. This exercise works the whole abdominal area.

DORSAL RAISES, or back arches. Lying on your front, push up with forearms remaining on the floor. Another way is to interlock your arms under your forehead and raise both arms and legs slowly, then lower to the floor again.

HEEL/CALF RAISES. A simple raise onto the toes, which can be executed at any time during the day. Use some support to keep balanced. To increase the effort, put a book or a block of wood under the toes.

HOPPING. There are a whole range of hopping exercises, from side to side or over a block of wood.

SQUATS. Do these with a chair behind the knees in order to ensure the knee does not go beyond 90° of flexion.

LEG RAISES. Sit on a chair (or the edge of a table), and bring the legs up to the horizontal. Work through the movement slowly. To add more resistance, try the exercise with a sock attached round the ankle, filled with about two pounds of weight, e.g. sand, salt or sugar. Even try this exercise with your newly purchased ski boots!

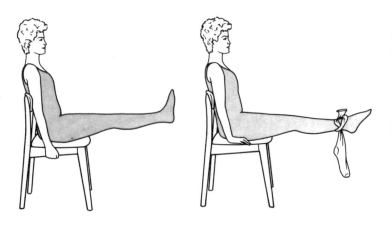

Glossary

Abonnement	Season ticket for lifts or lessons (the French term).
Aerials	A freestyle event of acrobatic ski jumping; performed off specially prepared "kickers".
Alpine Skiing	The term which distinguishes downhill skiing from the cross-country (Nordic) variety.
Angulation	A posture which enables the skier to control the skid of the skis by maintaining the upper body position away from the slope while pushing the knees and hips into the slope. Otherwise known as the banana shape.
Anti-friction pad	A pad behind the binding toe-piece which ensures the efficient release of the boot.
Anti-gliss	Ski-wear fabric which aims to reduce the slippery quality of ski clothes during a fall.
Après-ski	The evening fun.
Avalanche	The slide of snow down a mountainside after it has become unstable.
Avalement	A technique for absorbing bumps by leg and hip flexion, also used for starting some turns (e.g. Jet turns).
Backscratcher	A graphic description of a freestyle jump in which the skier remains upright while his ski tips point down and the ski tails are vertical behind his back.
Ballet	A freestyle discipline involving jumps, spins and somersaults with dance movements to music.
Banana	See Angulation.
BASI	British Association of Ski Instructors.
Basic swing	A turn initiated whilst ploughing but with the skis becoming parallel; the first downhill turn a beginner learns that introduces parallel skidding technique.
Basket	The metal or plastic disc near the bottom of a ski pole, which stops the pole tip going too far into the snow.
Biathlon	A Nordic event which combines the elements of cross-country racing and target shooting.
Binding	The means of attaching the boot to the ski, usually in two parts with a toe and a heel section.
Black Run	The grading for the most difficult and steepest of the marked runs at ski resorts.

Blood Wagon	The nickname for the stretcher-cum-sledge which is used by ski patrols to carry injured skiers down the mountain.
Blue Run	In a resort grading system blue is one of the easier runs (unless there are green runs, blue is the most simple).
Breakable Crust	The description of hazardous "off-piste" snow conditions where a hard frozen surface layer covers soft snow beneath.
Bubble	A type of lift/gondola.
Bumbag	A small pack worn at the waist on a belt.
Button Lift	A type of drag lift for one person. Often called a Poma after the manufacturer. Skiers are pulled uphill on button seats, supported from a cable by long metal rods. Also known as a pommel lift.
Cable Car	A large cabin lift suspended from a cable which is used to span high altitudes and wide chasms.
Camber	The arched shape of a ski in profile.
Canting	Compensating for a skier's knock knees or bow legs, to allow his skis to run flat on the snow. It is usually achieved with wedges between the skis and the bindings, but many boots have sole adjustments to create the required effect.
Carved Turn	A turn with no skidding, which produces a grooved track.
Chair Lift	A lift, suspended from an overhead cable, which carries skiers on seats.
Chill Factor	A theoretical temperature that tries to measure the impact on the human body of the combination of air temperature and air speed. Also called wind chill.
Christie	The name, deriving from the Norwegian town of Christiania, for any turn which allows the skis to skid; e.g. the stem christie where the outside ski stems out in a wedge form and the inner ski follows it and both skid whilst parallel.
Clip Boot	The usual name for the traditional front-entry style of Alpine ski boot.
Compression	A section of a course where the slope flattens out.
Compression Turn	The turn used when skiing moguls by flexing the legs to absorb the troughs and bumps.
Cornice	An overhanging ridge of wind-blown snow.
Corn Snow	See Spring Snow.
Cossack	A freestyle jump in which the legs are spread-eagled in a piked position.
Couloir	A narrow descent of extreme steepness.
Crevasse	A crack in a glacier. The fissure can extend hundreds of feet, and is often covered by snow.
Cross Country	Another name for Nordic skiing or *langlauf*, and separate from the Alpine downhill version. Cross-country skiers trek and travel uphill, downhill and on the flat.
Crud	A descriptive term for difficult heavy snow conditions.
Crust	A hard icy snow surface formed through continued melting and refreezing, but often not strong enough to support a skier's weight.
Daffy	A freestyle jump with one leg thrust forward and one leg back. In profile it looks like the furthest extension of a walking pace.
Dendix Slope	The brand name of many PVC brush artificial ski slopes.
DIN	(*Deutsche Industrie Norm.*) The German industrial standards by which many ski equipment quality controls are measured, especially with respect to binding release values.
Double Pole push	A technique which is applicable to both Alpine and cross-country skiing.

	Skiers use both poles, planted simultaneously in the snow, to propel themselves forward.
Downhill	One of the earliest and purest of the Alpine events. The race is decided over a course with relatively few control gates. The fastest skier wins.
Drag Lift	These come in two typical forms: the T-bar and the button lift. In all cases the skier is pulled uphill on skis using some fitment which is attached to an overhead cable.
Dry Slope	A form of artificial surface, usually either bristle or plastic-lattice, which tries to recreate the characteristics of skiing on snow.
Edging	Tilting the edge of one or both skis into the snow, to check sideways movement when traversing or to create a turn.
Fall Line	The steepest, shortest, most direct line down a slope.
FIS	*Fédération Internationale du Ski* (International Ski Federation), the ruling body of Alpine skiing.
Flexion	Any bending of a joint, as at ankles, knees, hips.
Flying Kilometre	A speed-skiing contest over a measured distance.
Foam Injection	A technique which forces foam into the inner boot; it moulds the boot to the foot in the hope of a comfortable fit.
Forfait	Package offered by resort covering accommodation, lift pass, ski school and perhaps ski hire, but not transport to the resort (the French term).
Freestyle Skiing	One of the newest skiing competitions. There are three disciplines: aerials, moguls and ballet.
Funicular	A mountain railway designed to travel up steep inclines.
Gaiter	A waterproof covering around the bottom of the trouser to keep snow out of the boot.
Gate	The device or checkpoint through which a skier must pass during a downhill or slalom race. It is made up of a pair of poles or flags.
Giant Slalom	One of the four Alpine racing disciplines, devised to test both the competitor's speed and turning technique.
Gilet	A padded waistcoat. Many new ski-jacket designs incorporate detachable sleeves to allow the garment to be converted into a gilet.
Glacier	A "river" of ice which can occupy entire valleys. A glacier is fed by accumulation of snow on high ground, and shows cycles of contraction and growth. Some resorts at high levels, with year-round snow cover, have developed summer skiing on local glaciers.
Glide Wax	A wax preparation for cross-country skis to reduce friction and allow the skis to slide more easily.
Glühwein	The German term for a hot spicy wine, known in Italy as *vino caldo* or in France as *vin chaud*.
Gondola	A lift system which incorporates a series of small cabins suspended from an overhead cable. They are also known as "bubbles" and in France as *télécabines*.
Green Run	In a resort grading system, green is the easiest ski run.
Grip Wax	A type of wax for cross-country skis to enhance grip on the snow, especially when climbing uphill or pushing off on the flat.
Haute Route	The paramount ski tour across the Alps from Argentière in France to Saas Fee in Switzerland.
Helicopter	A freestyle jump in which the skier remains upright while spinning through one or two rotations.

Heli-skiing	The use of helicopters as transport to off-piste runs. It is more common in North America.
Herringbone	A cross-country technique for climbing relatively easy slopes. Stepping up the hill the ski tips form the wider part of a wedge while the tails form the apex, rather like a reversed snowplough.
Hot Dogging	American term for freestyle mogul skiing.
Inner Boot	The soft cushioned lining to the outer rigid Alpine ski boot. It ensures insulation and a more comfortable fit.
Inside Ski	The ski nearest the centre of the arc when turning.
Jet Turn	A turn which is initiated by bending the hips and knees while pushing the feet forward to unweight the ski tips. Particularly useful as an athletic and aggressive method of turning over moguls.
Jump Turn	A turn used in steep or difficult conditions, in which the skier jumps and rotates the skis to effect a parallel turn into each traverse.
Kangaroo Turn	An extreme movement used to initiate a turn by sitting back.
Kicker	The ramp used by freestyle aerial jumpers.
Kick Turn	A method of turning through 180° from a standstill. First one ski is turned by pivoting it on its tail, then the second is swung round to reform the parallel position.
Klister	A type of soft wax applied to the base of a cross-country ski to make it grip the snow.
Langlauf	Cross-country skiing (the German term).
Loipe	A cross-country ski circuit, usually one prepared with machine-cut parallel tracks.
Mogul	A large bump in a ski run caused by successive skiers turning down the same line.
Mogul Field	A ski run which has been left to accumulate a series of moguls.
Moguls	The freestyle event which is contested down a mogul field. Skiers are marked on the quality of their turns through the fall line along with the speed of their descent and the height and difficulty of their jumps.
Mule kick	A freestyle jump which is similar to the backscratcher but the skis are held to the side of the body.
Nordic Skiing	The overall title for the competition disciplines of cross-country skiing and ski jumping (as opposed to Alpine skiing).
Nursery Slope	A slope of very gentle gradient where beginners can learn.
Off-Piste	A ski run which has not been prepared, graded or marked.
Outside Ski	The outer of the two skis whilst travelling around the arc of a turn.
Parallel Swing	A turn which is performed with the skis remaining parallel throughout.
Parapente	A parachute-cum-sail which is designed to permit simple steering manoeuvres. Those with skill and much fortitude use them to fly off the top of mountains.
Piste	A ski run which has been prepared and marked, and is regularly patrolled. Each piste is graded according to its steepness and difficulty. The hardest are signified by the colour black, below which come red, blue and (the easiest) green.
Piste Basher	Nickname for a tracked bulldozer used to flatten and groom the ski runs.
Piste Map	The printed plan of the lift systems, mountain huts, restaurants and ski runs (with their colour-coded degree of difficulty). No skier should leave home without one!

Pisteur	A member of the resort ski patrol.
Pole Flip	A freestyle ballet manoeuvre using the ski poles to execute a 360° flip over the poles.
Poma	A term for a button lift, abbreviated from Pomagalski, the name of the inventor and of the French manufacturing company.
Porridge	A reference to the type of snow which is wet, heavy and sticky.
Powder Snow	Light, dry, newly fallen snow which has not yet compacted.
Pulk	A sledge-and-harness device designed to be pulled by a cross-country skier; used especially in Scandinavia.
P-Tex	The brand name of a waxy plastic material which can be used to fill in gouges in the ski sole.
Ratrac	A piste preparation vehicle (otherwise known as a piste basher or snow cat); from the name of the original Swiss manufacturer.
Rear-Entry Ski Boot	An increasingly popular design of Alpine ski boot which opens at the back, as opposed to the traditional front-entry "clip" boot.
Red Run	In the resort grading of ski runs, red is intermediate to difficult.
Rollerski	A type of ski set on wheels to allow summer training for cross-country skiers.
Running Groove	The channel which runs down the length of a ski base and keeps the ski stable over the snow.
Running Surface	The base of the ski.
Running Wax	Preparation used on the base of a waxable cross-country ski, and coming in two types: grip wax to increase friction on the snow, and glide wax to reduce friction and allow the ski to slide more easily.
Salopettes	Waterproof ski dungarees.
Schuss	A descent straight down the fall line.
Short Swing	A short radius turn with the skis remaining parallel.
Shovel	The front of the ski at its widest point.
Side-Cut	The narrowing at the mid-section of a ski which forms its waist.
Side-Slip	A method of descending a slope by a controlled slipping motion of the skis.
Side-Step	The technique of ascending a hill by stepping sideways up the slope.
Ski-Brake	A brake mechanism (consisting of two prongs) which is released when a boot comes out of its binding and prevents the ski running off out of control. Also known as a Ski stopper.
Ski de Fond	Cross-country skiing (the French term).
Ski-Do	A motorcycle on skis (from the name of the manufacturer). The machine is driven by a caterpillar track at the rear, and steered by a pair of skis at the front.
Ski évolutif	A style of teaching in some areas of France which starts the beginner on very short skis before gradually progressing to a standard length.
Ski Stopper	See Ski-Brake
Ski Touring	The activity in which gentle mountaineering, cross-country skiing and Alpine downhill skiing unite.
Skins	Synthetic strips which can be tied or stuck to the base of cross-country touring skis or Alpine mountaineering skis, to enable skiers to walk up mountains. Seal skins used to be used, hence the name.
Slalom	One of the four Alpine ski racing disciplines and one of the most technical. It requires the skier to turn through tightly spaced gates over a steep half-kilometre course.

Snowboarding	A cross between skiing and surfing.
Snow Bridge	A bridge of snow across a crevasse in a glacier.
Snow Cat	Another term for "piste basher".
Snow-Chains	Essential for all car drivers heading for a ski resort. The chains wrap round the tyres to enable the car wheels to grip in the snow.
Snowploughing	The basic building block for controlled skiing. With tips together and tails apart the skis form a wedge shape. From this position the skier turns by putting pressure on one or other of the skis.
Speed Skiing	A competition to produce the fastest straight line speed, usually over the Flying Kilometre.
Spread Eagle	A freestyle jump in which the skier stays in an upright position while arms and legs are stretched out in a star shape.
Spring Snow	The conditions typical of spring, when the snow is reduced to icy granules from continued freeze-thaw. It is also known as corn snow.
Stem	Any move in which one or both of the skis is fanned out to initiate a turn, with the skis then returning to parallel.
Step Turn	A parallel turn which is initiated by an uphill step.
Stick Wax	A type of hard wax applied to the base of a cross-country ski to make it grip the snow.
Sun Crust	The surface crust formed by melted and refrozen snow.
Super-Giant	The newest of the four Alpine ski events, a cross between the downhill and the giant slalom. Also known as super-G.
Swing	A ski turn.
Tail	The rear end of a ski.
T-Bar	The original design for a drag lift to pull two people uphill.
Télécabine	A gondola (the French term).
Téléférique	A cable car (the French term).
Telemark	A method of turning downhill on cross-country skis, with their toe-only bindings. Mainly used in ski touring and in telemark slalom racing (telemarking).
Tip	The front end of a ski.
Tip Roll	A freestyle ballet manoeuvre in which the skier pirouettes over the ski tips.
Touring Binding	A variable binding which allows the heel to be either fixed or released so enabling the skier to ski downhill or climb.
Traverse	A skier's direction across a slope as opposed to down the fall line.
Tuck	An aerodynamic crouched position adopted by skiers when schussing. It is especially effective for speed skiers.
Unweighting	The method of taking weight off a ski to prepare for a turn more easily.
Waist	The mid-section where a ski is at its narrowest and thickest.
Wash-Board	A series of equally spaced bumps/ridges caused by skiers taking the same path.
Wedel	A German expression for performing linked very short radius turns down the fall line with the upper body steady and using flat or nearly flat skis.
Wedge	Another name for the snowplough.
White-Out	A term which refers to a drastic reduction in visibility (possibly even impairing a skier's sense of direction) caused by low cloud, falling snow or fog.
Wind Chill	See Chill Factor

Wind Crust	Snow condition on windward slopes where the snow hardens to a crust and is etched by the wind.
Wind Slab	Snow which has been deposited on the leeward side of slopes by strong winds. It becomes hard and unstable and poses the threat of avalanche.
Wipe Out	A dramatic fall! Happy landings!

Useful Addresses

Ski Club of Great Britain

There are now 22,000 members of the Ski Club of Great Britain which was established in 1903. Since then it has been at the forefront of skiing. The club offers a package of benefits including a discount card recognized by more than 50 ski tour operators and over 100 ski shops around Britain as well as many more in the Alps. There is also a comprehensive information service to help you plan your holidays, choose resorts and select equipment. There are the latest snow reports (telephone 0898 666777) and insurance packages, flights, mail order ski and après-ski items. They hold regular meetings, ski lectures, films and social events, both at their London headquarters and also around the country. They have resort reps at 334 different locations in the Alps who will ski with you and help you get the most out of your holiday. These reps are contactable through the Ski Club office or at the Tourist Offices in many European resorts.

Ski Club of Great Britain
118 Eaton Square
London SW1W 9AF
tel 071–245 1033

English Ski Council
6th Floor
Area Library Building
Halesowen
West Midlands
tel 021–501 2314

British Ski Club for the Disabled
Corton House
Corton
Warminster
Wiltshire BA12 0NZ

Ski Council of Wales
PO Box 3
Chepstow
Gwent NP5 6XJ
tel 0222 619637

British Ski Federation
Pyrford Road
West Byfleet
Surrey KT14 6RA
tel 0932 336488

The Uphill Ski Club of Great
Britain
12 Park Crescent
London W1N 4EQ

Ulster Ski Council
43 Ballymaconnell Road
Bangor
County Down
Northern Ireland
tel 0247 473134

Back Up (Skier's charity which
supports all spinally injured
sportsmen and women)
Room 102
The Business Village
Broomhill Road
London SW18 4JQ
tel 081–871 5180

BASI
Inverdruie Visitors Centre
Grampian Road
Aviemore
Inverness-shire PH22 1QH
tel 0479 810407

N E Scotland Sports Association
60 Union Street
Keith
Banffshire AB5 3DP

North East Ski Association
2 Brierdene Road
Whitley Bay
Tyne and Wear

Scottish National Ski Council
Caledonia House
South Gyle
Edinburgh EH12
tel 031–317 7280

The Sports Council
16 Upper Woburn Place
London WC1H 0QP
tel 071–388 1277

Upski Ltd
Garden Cottages
High Close
Langdale
Ambleside
tel 09667 387

British Deaf Ski Club
16 Starling Close
Woose Hill
Wokingham
Berks

Ski Club of Ireland
Dublin Sport House
Kilterman
County Dublin

The British Ski Slope Operators
Association
Ski Rossendale
Haslingden Old Road
Rawtenstall
Rossendale BB4 8RR
tel 0706 228844

Association of British Ski
Operators
118 Eaton Square
London SW1W 9AF
tel 071–235 8227

Austria – Österreichischer
Skiverband
Olympiastrasse 10
Innsbruck A–6020
tel 05–222 221 43

France – Fédération Française du
Ski
50 rue des Marquisats
BP 451
74009 Annecy
tel 50 51 40 34

Switzerland – Fédération Suisse du
Ski
Schosshaldensstrasse 32
3000 Berue 32
tel 031–434/444

Index